JOWETT

A CENTURY OF MEMORIES

JOWETT

A CENTURY OF MEMORIES

NOEL STOKOE

AMBERLEY

To our dear grandchildren, Luke, Daisy, Jack and Oliver,
the 'Jowett Juniors'

First published 2010

Amberley Publishing Plc
Cirencester Road, Chalford,
Stroud, Gloucestershire, GL6 8PE

www.amberley-books.com

British Library Cataloguing in Publication Data.
A catalogue record for this book is available from the
British Library.

ISBN 978 1 4456 0087 1

Typeset in 10pt on 12pt Sabon.
Typesetting and Origination by Fonthill.
Printed in the UK.

CONTENTS

This is an interesting add from 1932, as the car was too heavy to sit on top of the boat, so they blew a photo up to the full size of the car, cut it out and stuck it onto the roof of the boat to look like the real thing – it seemed to fool everybody at the time!

ACKNOWLEDGEMENTS

Firstly, I must thank all the contributors for taking the trouble to contact me with their stories relating to Jowett cars after reading my requests for information in various publications. Clearly, there would be no book now if I had not received these first-hand accounts from them.

As with all my previous books, I would like to thank my wonderful wife, Jane, for her continued support and understanding for all things Jowett. Special thanks to Tony Fearn for his invaluable support in proof-reading this book for me.

Other titles by Noel Stokoe:

Jowett 1901-1954 (Images of Motoring), ISBN: 0752417231
My Car was a Jowett, ISBN: 0752427960
Jowett – Advertising the Marque, ISBN: 0752435353
Sporting Jowetts, ISBN: 9780752447759

"BLACKBIRD" and "KINGFISHER"

SHORT SALOONS DE-LUXE

WITH FOUR-WHEEL BRAKES AND TWO DOORS

An entirely new body of advanced design, incorporating sliding roof, winding windows to doors and quarter lights.　Chromium plated one-piece opening screen of safety glass, rear petrol tank, petrol pump, petrol gauge, clock and speedometer, automatic ignition and warning light.　Cellulose finish.

"Blackbird"　　Black with green beading, interior in shaded blue rexine or fawn moquette.

"Kingfisher"　　Blue with light blue beading and interior as above.

For full specification see page 18.

Price, Coachbuilt only, £150 (ex works)

JOWETT CARS LIMITED · IDLE · BRADFORD · YORKS ·

INTRODUCTION

The year 2010 is a real milestone in Jowett circles, as it marks the centenary of Jowett car production. The Jowett brothers, William and Benjamin, built their first prototype car in 1906, which they ran and tested until 1910. By that time, they felt that the car was ready to go into production; these first cars were all fitted with the flat-twin horizontally opposed 'little engine with the big pull'. By 1916, a total of forty-eight cars had been built, but production then ceased in favour of munitions work for the First World War effort.

Manufacture started again in 1920 at a new purpose-built factory at Five Lane Ends, Idle, Bradford, when production volumes increased dramatically. As described in my previous books and in various other Jowett history books, the Jowett brothers carried on producing cars powered by the flat-twin engine with various body designs right through the 1920s and 1930s, but the range of

The 1½ litre Jowett JAVELIN

IT'S NEW RIGHT THROUGH

cars and vans was joined by a flat-four engine in 1935. Both engine types were produced right up to the outbreak of the Second World War in 1939, but once again, production was switched over to the war effort.

After the war, the motoring world was taken by storm by the Gerald Palmer masterpiece, the Javelin saloon, soon to be followed by the Jupiter sportscar. These cars were such a departure for Jowett after the ultra-reliable, thrifty pre-war models; what a shame it all came to a rapid end in 1954. Jowetts still have a very strong following, with enthusiasts all over the world, even though it is now fifty-six years since the production lines ceased.

I have been collecting people's first-hand reminiscences for over twenty-five years, and my second book, *My Car was a Jowett*, was a collection of over 100 of them. This book is a further selection of memories of ex-Jowett owners, drivers and workers, which I hope you will enjoy reading as much as I enjoyed receiving them. Over the years, I have published many letters in the club magazine, *The Jowetteer*, but there have been so many, it would be impossible to publish all of them, so I am delighted to reproduce a further selection of them here.

The book is brought up to date with a selection of colour photos I took at the Jowett Centenary Rally, which was held in Wakefield over the Bank Holiday weekend 28-31 May 2010.

MEMORIES OF
EX-JOWETT EMPLOYEES

LONG-TERM JOWETT EMPLOYEE –
HARRY ESMOND GILL

After reading the article 'The glory days of Jowett' which was published in the October 2009 issue of the *Dalesman* magazine, I am writing to tell you about my father.

Harry Esmond Gill began at the Jowett factory in Idle, Bradford, in 1923 as a fourteen-year-old apprentice. He died many years ago, but carried out many duties whilst working for the Company. The following notes have been taken from his notebook which is now in my possession.

His first twelve months were passed in the Engine Testing Department, followed by work in various parts of the Assembly Shop. In 1929 he transferred to Rectification, road testing, finishing and final inspection; he also spent some time in the Service Department.

By 1939 the factory had switched to munitions work and he was in charge of a department housed in the Bradford Power Station. Here they dealt with the repair and assembly of Air Force ground equipment, including bomb trolleys.

After the war he assisted in the development of the Bradford van and the Javelin prototypes. Then, as foreman of finished cars, he went on the road to test Jupiters in chassis form, for 100 miles each.

By the end of car production in 1953, he was working in the Service Department, repairing crashed and damaged cars and servicing them.

In 1954 he was offered a new job with Cyclemaster Ltd in Battersea. I understand that the Manager and some of the Directors were previously involved with Jowett Cars Ltd.

As regards the Jupiter testing routes, when I look at the map and trace the familiar names, it makes me think that he varied the route which he took, but must have known Yorkshire very well. We were living on Wrose Road, Bradford, then and one trip would have been out towards Skipton, Settle, Austwick, Kirkby

Lonsdale, Catterick, Ripon, Harrogate, Guiseley and back to Shipley. Another way which seems familiar is Baildon, Ilkley, Bolton Abbey, Kilnsey, Aysgarth, Hawes, Ingleton, Skipton and back. On one occasion I remember coming to Whitby in a car on test going past Fylingdales early warning station which was just visible through the mist and the cold, but I am sorry to say I do not remember the type of Jowett it was. You will see from the enclosed newspaper clipping that he was in trouble for speeding whilst driving one of the Jupiter chassis, which was very worrying and embarrassing for him at the time, and resulted in a fine for him.

Both Joyce (my sister) and I remember going to the ' family' days, which were organised by Jowetts for the workers. Fruit and vegetables were sold off at the end of the day and we did coloured pictures for the colouring competition. We also played on bomb trolleys but I do not remember where that was.

Our house on Wrose Road was not far from the factory so we went there fairly frequently. In later years we lived at Bolton Villas and left there to live in Woking, Surrey, when the factory closed down. Mum and Dad emigrated as £10 Poms to Australia in the late 1960s. I did not see them again after they left for Australia. My children were young and there was no money for travel. It seems that Australia was too hot for them and Dad could not find satisfactory work. After going on holiday to New Zealand they liked that better and settled in Levin on the North Island. I do remember some correspondence about Jowetts there; it may have involved a Club. If we had PCs then it would have been so much easier to keep in contact.

As youngsters, we always remember having a car of some kind and going on camping holidays when many people did not have holidays.

When we left our bungalow in Surrey and moved to Norfolk in 1999 and cleared out the loft many interesting things were revealed. Along with four artificial Christmas trees, books and old records, there was Dad's American sheepskin flying jacket complete with bullet hole and electrical heating wires. He used to wear it when out on Jupiter chassis testing in the cold weather. When my brother visited from America I gave it to him to take back there. He also wore an all-in-one padded zip-up garment which had not survived so well in the roof. The sheepskin jacket must have belonged to an American stationed here, but how Dad acquired it I do not know. I was just thinking that he would have been 101 years old last week.

How interesting that one of the cars we went out in was a Monte Carlo Rally entrant. I think we were too young to know about that sort of thing. Mum and Dad probably discussed events and we did not realise the significance. He often brought cars home and we would go out for a weekend ride but whether this was for testing purposes or just a loan so we could go out somewhere I do not know.

We went to the Festival of Britain in 1951 in a Javelin but so far I have not found pictures of that. We stayed with friends of the family who lived in Harrow, and we (four children) slept on the floor.

You would have liked our Dad; he could do most things associated with cars. Brian, my brother, takes after him and has totally rebuilt E-Type Jaguars, one just from parts.

Dad always carried everything needed for repairs and also a fire extinguisher. This was used on one memorable occasion when flames shot up from the engine when he folded back the covers. It was probably the old Jowett registered BV4678 as this was our family car when we were small.

Some of my old pictures are of Dad with cars which may or may not be Jowetts, I will send them anyway. I know that his father, who had a wholesale grocery business in Bradford, had some of the very early cars.

Jeanne and Joyce Gill standing next to a Javelin registered FKW318, which was an early example (probably 1948), parked outside the Gill's home.

I enclose a photograph of him with a Bradford van, but I am not sure which year it was taken. I also have pictures of him with other cars, but I am not sure if they are Jowetts or not.

You may find this a bit jumbled but it was a long time ago. I will be seventy-three this year; the others are all younger. Brian is the next one down and probably remembers more. We went out in cars all the time when not many families had them. They broke down often but Dad always had the right 'bit' tucked away and was able to get us home.

Mrs Jeanne Bexley ... Attleborough, Norfolk, January 2010

Harry Gill inspects an early Bradford van at the factory; this is an early example with separate sidelights fitted.

A rare unofficial photo of Harry Gill on the Javelin production line.

Above and below: A youthful-looking Harry Gill with his father's 1920s Long-Four.

The Gill family car: a Javelin registered HKU638. This was a 1951 example.

This Javelin, registered EPR999, was of particular interest to me, as this is the car that Bob Foster and George Holdsworth drove in the 1952 Monte Carlo Rally! I asked Jeanne about this and she said that her father regularly came home in cars he was testing at the time!

Harry Gill and his son, Brian, at the wheel of a Jupiter chassis on test. Every Jupiter was taken out on a 100-mile test in chassis form prior to completion. Mr Gill used to dress in an American airman's leather flying jacket and an all-in-one thermal-type boiler suit in cold weather. He also had the embarrassment of being prosecuted for speeding whilst driving one in a built-up area!

A Jupiter out on test with Harry Gill on trade plates at an unknown location.

Harry Gill sits in one of the 1952 Le Mans R1 Jupiters at the back of the factory. A team of three R1s were entered at Le Mans that year, but only one finished the twenty-four-hour race, but it managed to win the 1½-litre class again, making it a hat-trick of wins in 1950, 1951 and 1952. This car can be recognised as a 1952 car, as it has faired-in front wings; the sole 1951 R1 car had the motorcycle-type wings.

CHIEF CAR TESTER AT OTLEY COURT

Conditionally discharged for speeding

Harry E. Gill, Clare Road, Bolton Villas, Bradford, said to be chief tester for Jowett cars, was conditionally discharged at Otley today for exceeding the speed limit while driving a Jowett Jupiter chassis.

Chief Insp. Glasspool read a letter from Jowett Cars, Ltd., which stated that Gill had been chief tester for 20 years. At the time he had been driving a high-performance chassis intended for export to America on which rigorous tests had to be made. Gill admitted driving at 45 to 50 m.p.h.

The newspaper clipping referring to Harry Gill speeding on a Jupiter chassis.

MEMORIES OF HORACE GRIMLEY

I have recently received a copy of the *Dalesman* magazine (sent to me by an Aunt) in which there is your article on the Jowett Jupiter. I found it very interesting indeed as I was at Le Mans in 1950 when the first Jupiter raced there and won its class. It was very heady stuff for a seventeen-year-old, as I was then. My father manufactured springs for Jowetts, and as we lived nearby, knew Willie Jowett very well.

I learnt to drive in a Jowett Javelin and was taught by Horace Grimley, another friend of my father and, I believe, a nephew to Willie Jowett. He also drove in the Monte Carlo Rally, first in a Javelin and later in a Jupiter. I also seem to remember he came round to our house once with a Farina-bodied Jupiter coupe prior to it being exported to take part in another Rally. [*This will have been Marcel Becquart's car, which he drove in the 1952 & 1953 Monte Carlo Rally ... NS*]. I think that there were only four made, and I drove it before and after the Rally, but it was a bit of a wreck afterwards!

It was very exciting in the pits at Le Mans, as Fangio was there that year. He was a very mild man and a very careful driver on the circuit and on the open road. I think that it was the Fiats that were the main rivals of the Jupiter, but one by one during the night their engines blew up. There was wild rejoicing each time this happened, but the whole pits area seemed to rejoice when 'our team' won. The car was called the *Sagacious II*, which I think was a play on the drivers' names; they were Tommy Wise and Tommy Wisdom. I have a photo of the car in the pits with Charles Grandfield and Horace Grimley and, incidentally, myself well in the background and heavily disguised in sun specs. I will certainly have this copied for you and send you a copy, if you would like it. [*You bet! I did in fact use the picture in my first book* Jowett 1901-1954 *... NS*].

Thank you again for your article, it brought back so many happy memories for me, I can well remember the excitement of going to Le Mans, my father took our Javelin to the works at Idle to have the suspension adjusted in readiness for the rough French roads.

One other small snippet I can tell you about the Le Mans Jupiter was whilst in the race it developed a leaking petrol or hydraulic pipe, which was temporarily replaced with chewing gum (I have carried chewing gum in my car ever since) and we had to drive into the town of Le Mans itself to obtain a spare, which was smuggled into the car down the trousers of the next driver to be 'discovered' in the car the next time the car came into the pits. This had to be done as the car was only allowed to use the spares it was carrying or what had been approved beforehand to be in the pits. I wonder if you knew that – I bet you didn't as it was obviously not talked about at the time as the car could have been disqualified!

I do not know if my mother has any other photographs, but I hope to visit her later in the year; she still lives in Yorkshire and we are coming over to see her, so will look if you are interested. Also if you would like a copy of the picture that I have, please let me know.

Mrs Deborah Cargill ... Tare, New South Wales, Australia, June 1991

Well, how was that for a letter out of the blue! Needless to say I wrote back to Deborah asking for a copy of the picture and also for any other memories she may have of the Jowett factory and the personalities, such as Horace Grimley and Charles Grandfield. The reply she sent me was more than I could have hoped for, as there was so much more interesting information detailed. The only disappointment was that no other photographs were found, and she had no record of her father's Javelin ... but I should not be so greedy!

I was very pleased indeed to receive your letter and the booklet on Jowett cars. It arrived at a busy time for me as it was our financial year end, so I apologise for the slight delay in replying to you. I can assure you that I have had the time to read and re-read your letter and book, I am delighted to think you have sent me the last copy that you have, but I will treasure it always. And, having just got my bank reconciliations out of the way I feel I now have time to lift my nose from the grindstone long enough to answer your letter. It was a string of the strangest coincidences that prompted me to write to you in the first place, and how pleased I am that I did. [*Not as pleased as I was! ... NS*].

I am afraid that I will be a disappointment to you in recalling memories of Le Mans in 1950; at that time in my life I was more interested in the two-legged talent wearing trousers than four-wheeled talent clad in rubber! I can, however, tell you that I was also at the Ulster TT race at Dundrod with my parents, but the only things I can remember about that was the appalling weather, the fact that it was Stirling Moss's twenty-first birthday and that it was the first time in my life that I was served with two chops on my plate, as England was still in the throws of post-war shortages. I do recall a much livelier after race celebration than at Le Mans, where everyone fell slowly but surely to sleep after the latter.

I loved the photo of Horace at the wheel of the Jupiter; you are quite right in saying that he was a kind mild-mannered man, as he most surely was. It seemed likely after my first driving lesson with my father that he was not the teacher for me and my second lesson only confirmed this! I cannot remember how it came about, but Horace finished up taking over my tuition, which must have been an awful drag for him, but it was the best thing that ever happened to me. Not only was he an excellent driver, he was a super tutor as well, with all the patience in the world. Every Thursday night, come rain, hail, snow or fog, he would arrive round at our house in his left-hand-drive Javelin '777', park up in front of the house and go off with me in my father's Javelin. Some nights the weather conditions were dreadful, but no pleas from me would make him relent, he reckoned I might get caught in bad driving conditions and had to learn how to handle them. One night I got lost in thick fog, we used to have some real beauties in industrial Yorkshire in those days, and when I asked for help all he would say was he would not always be in the passenger seat, and what would I do if he wasn't there. So I followed a bus on the assumption that it would lead me to somewhere: it did, right into a very brightly lit Huddersfield Bus Depot, which I might add was much to Horace's amusement.

One of his tips was to enter a left-hand bend wide if driving conditions permitted, and this was one of his tips I passed on to my son when I taught him to drive, and having what I think we should add nerves of steel to Horace's qualities! Having passed his test while in his final year at school he had the opportunity to go on to an advanced driver's course at Amaroo Park. So off he went in my car which was one of the last Mini Cooper S, and proceeded to beat the pants off his school mates. The instructor asked him who had taught him apex cornering. Up until that time I had no idea what they called Horace's cornering techniques, so you see his spirit still lives on.

Horace and his wife Muriel, Charles and Annie Grandfield, Roy and Jeannie Lunn were all frequent visitors at our home, but most particularly Horace. His postcard to me at college from Monte Carlo at the end of the rally was a great boost to my popularity. But to be a successful rally and racing driver I think that you need aggression and the ability to mistreat the vehicle, and he certainly lacked both. My father loved his two Javelins. Horace did not want him to buy his first one as it had only been driven previously by professional drivers; he reckoned it took the ordinary driver to find out the latent faults, and he was right. The second Javelin did not give anything like the same amount of trouble as the first one did, which reminds me of another maxim of Horace's – 'Never buy the first model, let others find out the car's weaknesses first!'

As regards the Farina-bodied Jupiter, I was interested to hear that there were four and not the two that I had stated in my first letter. I still remember when Horace brought round a brand new one to Spring Bank, our home, and let me have a little drive in it before it set off for the Monte Carlo Rally. He brought it round again after the rally so I could have another drive in it – boy was that car shot at, Horace wanted me to see the difference in the car after a hard rally.

My father's firm was Joseph Steel & Sons of Harden, near Bingley; my father died before Horace and after his death the firm was eventually taken over by Woodheads who in turn were taken over by Carclo Engineering. I must confess I have no idea as to which models of Jowett our springs were used on, but I would suspect it would have been most of them. The internal combustion engine is almost a complete mystery to me. I had to do a certain amount of theory when I took my now lapsed private pilot's license many years ago; the only thing I can remember of that now is that radial engines had to have an odd number of cylinders. It was a bit like my Latin: learnt it to pass the exam and then promptly forgotten.

The Jupiter on the front cover of the booklet you sent me looked good enough to eat. I just wish I had worn so well; perhaps I need a restoration job too! As requested, I am enclosing the Le Mans picture for you to copy which shows the back view of Horace, Charles Grandfield and a scrutineer by the car and Tommy Wisdom, me and an unknown in the pits – I'm the one in the dress in the background, but I look more like the bloke with a towel nowadays.

I'm not surprised by the way that Roy Lunn is hardly in the Le Mans photo – he wasn't supposed to be there! He'd chartered a plane from Yeadon and flown in. Charles Grandfield was furious; accommodation was somewhat scarce at Le Mans and he finished up bunking in with the two Tommys as I recall.

He was a lively character and caused both Tommys to be late for the celebration dinner by pouring an urn of what Roy thought was cold water over the pair of them having a well-earned soak in the bath. The contents turned out to be soil and they had the devil's own job getting it out of the bath with its very peculiar plughole; well, at least that was their story! But I well remember taking a stroll along part of the course with Roy just after he'd arrived to let Charles cool off a bit.

As you can see, your letter and booklet gave me much pleasure and did indeed bring back many happy memories, and I do hope you will forgive this verbal diarrhoea, and I will certainly get in touch if I manage to get over to England this year. Many thanks indeed Noel for re-awakening these memories for me, but weren't you a naughty boy taking a Jupiter onto the sands at Sandsend with all that salt, but I suppose if they still salt the roads in England there is not much difference!

I returned the photo to Deborah after I copied it, but sadly that was the last contact I had with her. As regards her verbal diarrhoea, nothing could have been further from the truth, as there were so many super stories she had to tell; in fact,

I would have loved to have kept in contact with her better. With regards to the 'naughty photo' of me with my Jupiter on the beach at Sandsend, it was not quite what it seemed. The picture was used in the Dalesman magazine to illustrate my article on the Jupiter's fortieth anniversary. I had driven the car down a concrete slipway that led down to the beach; the picture was printed in black and white, which made it look like the car was on the sand, but the car was still safely parked on the concrete slipway!

MORE MEMORIES OF HORACE GRIMLEY

I was about to send the manuscript of this book to my publishers when I received an email from Vandon Grimley, Horace's grandson, enclosing a super picture of a family camping holiday.

My Uncle Steven came to visit us recently. He brought some old pictures with him, most of which I'd not seen before. I thought you might be interested in this one (attached). It is in Normandy near Guildford, Surrey, in the early 1960s. Horace Grimley stands near his Javelin and Sprite caravan. His son Victor (my dad) is facing him. My brother Marcus is in the toy car and I'm on the toy tractor. Horace and Muriel (my grandma) would often travel from Bradford to Normandy to take us on holiday in the caravan.

Hope to catch up with you again some time.

Vandon Grimley ... May 2010

Needless to say, I wrote back in the hope there may have been more pictures ...

Thank you for your reply. My grandpa had a very calm nature about him. I can only remember him being displeased on one occasion. This was when my brother and I (sitting in the back of the Javelin while towing the caravan) started bouncing up and down in unison. This must have upset the 'rig' and could have sent it out of control.

It would be wonderful to see the family picture in your latest book. Please do feel free to put it in. I have enclosed five more of Steven's pictures. I hope the file won't clog up your system while it transfers! In the first picture I think my grandma stands in the doorway and one of the boys will be Steven. The next is Horace, Muriel and Steven (I think). On the next is Horace collecting water. The next will be in the Yorkshire Dales, and the last one is Horace watching someone working on a car, but where?

I hope you enjoy these. I am looking forward to the new book!

Vandon and Pauline Grimley ... May 2010

The Grimley family on their way to a camping holiday. They would regularly travel from Bradford. Horace is standing by the caravan and his son Victor is facing him. Victor's two boys are also in the picture: Marcus is in the toy car and Vandon is on the tractor.

A side view of Horace Grimley's Sprite caravan, it shows Horace's wife, Muriel, with one of their two grandsons, Marcus or Vandon, and the pet Cocker Spaniel.

Another view of Horace's Javelin and caravan. Horace ran this Javelin registered GKW770, which was a left-hand-drive car, for many years, right into the 1960s. The car does still exist, but has been stored for many years and is in a derelict state. In view of the car's history, I do hope that the car may at last be restored by its new owner.

This picture shows another view of Horace's Javelin and Sprite caravan, Vandon confirms that Horace had a very calm nature about him. He says that the only time he saw his grandfather displeased was when he and his brother, Marcus, were sitting on the back seat of the Javelin and were bouncing up and down in unison, they were told that this may upset the 'rig' and could have sent it out of control!

MEMORIES OF TOMMY WISE,
BY HIS DAUGHTER NIKKI

Just another of those strange coincidences – Crown Car Sales, Castle Road, Scarborough, was before that Crystal's Garage, and yes you have guessed it, Wise of Scarborough before that. In those days it was the Head Office of Pop's Company. He did not have it during the Jowett period, but it was the Jowett agency up until the closure of the Jowett factory. He had a garage in Harrogate at that time and was the Jowett agent there. When he bought the Scarborough premises he ran a Ford Dealership from there. The garage he had in Harrogate was situated behind the George Hotel and was called St Peter's Motors. At the time, we were living just outside Harrogate.

I remember once that he had to be in Scarborough in a bit of a hurry (an understatement if ever there was one!) to sign a contract on what was then Whittaker's Garage. I don't know if you remember the old road from Harrogate to Scarborough, but you had to go through Knaresborough along really wiggly roads full of treacherous corners etc. They used to reckon that it would take between 1½ – 2 hours, but Pop did it in 54 minutes (or so the story goes!) – in a Jowett of course! I'm trying to fathom out which one it would have been, but it would have been in late 1954 or early 1955 and I was too young to remember. Anyway, he made it in time for the meeting, and the rest is history as the say.

Nikki Wise … Snainton, Scarborough, June 1995

I used to see Nikki fairly regularly in the mid-1990s and would also send her copies of articles that mentioned her father. I also visited her house once to look at all Tommy's cups and memorabilia, which was a most enjoyable visit. This next letter from her was prompted by me sending her an article on Gerald Palmer (the Javelin's designer), which mentioned her father several times.

Thank you so much for the copy of the article written on Gerald Palmer – I hadn't seen it and I don't think my mother will have seen it either. It brought back a lot of memories of him telling his story, a lot of the details I would not have remembered and I certainly had not seen the pictures before.

You really are very kind to think of sending me all this information about Pop – some of which I didn't know, believe it or not! He wasn't a great one for telling us about things that were in the past; he always said, 'That was the past – think of now and the future.' I know how busy you are and it is greatly appreciated; it is also nice for Nick, as he never met my father or mother.

Nikki Wise … Snainton, Scarborough, February 1997

MEMORIES OF A JOWETT AGENCY EMPLOYEE

As a baby in 1937 I was often taken down in the Jowett to Green's Chemist to be weighed, I in fact still have the card with my weights on! At that time we were living in Duchy Avenue, Otley.

My mother worked at the Grosvenor Garage prior to her marriage and I have a picture of the garage with a car parked in front of the showroom with the registration number KY1 clearly visible. Also shown in the picture is a 7-hp Jowett two-seater reduced in price from £150 to £139 and deferred payments being available, if required!

Other items I still have relating to Jowetts are a 1910 Jowett lapel badge and a Thompson's Guide – price 3d!

My biggest regret is that when we sold our Javelin we sold it with its registration plate, GAK1, still on the car. [*That would be worth tens of thousands now … NS*]

I do hope these little snippets will be of interest to you.

Mrs Molly Laxton … Otley, North Yorkshire, January 2010

I had some very interesting correspondence from Mrs Molly Laxton telling me about her mother, who worked at Jowett agency in Bradford, The Jowett Manufacturing Company, prior to her marriage. This picture shows the garage with a 1931 Jowett saloon parked in front with the fantastic registration number KY1; I bet this will be on the Lord Mayor's car now!

Camping 1930s style! This is a publicity postcard that was given away by the Jowett Motor Manufacturing Company showing three very pretty young ladies making afternoon tea – happy days!

Molly Laxton's mother by the side of a 1931 saloon. I am not sure if this was a publicity shot or not, but it does have the charm and feel of the period.

Another, what looks to be, posed publicity shot of three young ladies preparing and starting a late-1920s Jowett saloon. Molly's mother is the girl in the middle.

Mr Shaw with his daughter, Molly, with the personal Javelin registered GAK1 (another Bradford registration). This is an early example with the one-piece chrome grille and small 5½-inch headlamps. Molly said that it was always her parents' regret in later years that they sold the Javelin still with its registration number, as clearly, even then, it was worth money, and would be worth thousands now.

SHORT SALOON DE-LUXE MODELS
WITH FOUR-WHEEL BRAKES AND TWO DOORS

These models have been introduced in response to a demand for an improved edition of the Standard Short Saloon, and for a more compact version of the Black Prince. In addition to the usual comprehensive equipment as provided with the standard models, a chromium plated, single pane, opening windscreen is fitted, and wire wheels of a superior type to those usually found on light cars. These last are finished in various shades to match the beading and tone with the colour of the car. The exterior fabric and interior trimming is of a superlative quality, and the steering wheel and gear lever knob are of a shade to match the decorations. The whole interior displays a perfect colour scheme. Upholstery is in either a high grade fabric or moquette, and the car gives a sense of luxury and well-being never before attained at this figure. Radiator, door handles and outside bright parts chromium plated.

Price £158 (ex works).

"Black Prince." Black with red or cream decorations. Interior in red fabric or moquette.

"Grey Knight." Grey with blue decorations. Interior in blue antique fabric or moquette to match.

"Silverdale." Fawn with brown decorations. Interior in brown antique fabric or moquette to match.

"Splintex" Glass all round   -   -   -   £7 . 10 : 0 extra.

MEMORIES OF EX-JOWETT RALLY DRIVERS

MONTE CARLO RALLY JAVELIN REGISTERED DJG1

It is true that George Fitt Motors were the Jowett Main Dealers for East Kent, but with the exception of the *Daily Express* Rallies, they were not financially involved with my competition work with my Javelin which was registered DJG1. My first event was the 1949 Monte Carlo Rally but ended up 101st as, having made excellent times in the test and first runs of the deciding tests, then I accidentally over-revved and got air into the hydraulic tappets which cut the power right down. I should have said at this point that the car was prepared for me in the Competition Department at the Jowett factory in Idle at their expense.

I also ran in the 1950 Monte Carlo Rally and we had heavy snow from Nevers until we ran downhill into Monte. Unfortunately my co-driver put the car halfway down a bank (in spite of my commands to halt, from the back seat) when trying to edge past a Dutch tourer which had pulled up as a lorry was facing it. We were luckily held up from overturning by a tree. With the help of the lorry and its driver we were able to extricate ourselves after a while and made it to the finish in the 100th position mark I believe.

I think it must have been in 1950 that I ran in the Alpine Rally and lost a blade off my fan and finally had the distributor soaked in a tremendous thunder storm which pushed me right out of contention, though I did get to Cortina. Horace Grimley crashed his car the next day, so we gave a lift to Gordon Wilkins, his co-driver, to Chamonix, a day which we shall remember, as the engine kept cutting out, and it was not until that evening that I managed to cure it. The same year I ran it in the first Production Car Race at Silverstone, but the edge had been taken off the performance of the car, as my mechanic had made a mess of the timing.

These are the inglorious tales of my major excursions, but among others, I did run in two or three *Daily Express* Rallies with a team of three Javelins entered by George Fitt Motors. The business was sold some years ago and is now extinct; there were no photographs taken at all by me and as far as I am aware no records of George Fitt Motors are left. All I could suggest is that you contact *The Whitstable Times* and perhaps *The Kent Messenger.*

Your club headed paper lists your Presidents and Vice Presidents, which brings back memories of forty years ago, as I knew George Green, Gerry Palmer, Charles Grandfield and Roy Lunn very well, not to mention dear old Horace Grimley, and was surprised that all the first named were still alive, for I am eighty-seven next month.

If I can help you with information in the future, do not hesitate to contact me and I shall be pleased to see you if you are ever in this area.

C. J. Turner ... Eastling, nr Faversham, June 1989

Twenty-one years on and everybody with the exception of Roy Lunn is long gone, but Roy goes from strength to strength. About fifteen years ago, the remains of Mr Turner's Javelin registered DJG1 were discovered in a very poor state of repair. This was, I think, the last remaining Monte Carlo Javelin survivor. The car was bought by a number plate dealer, who managed to transfer the plate off it even though there was no way on earth this car could have been restored and an MOT issued. I have always been told that a car had to hold an MOT and be on the road to have its number transferred off it, but clearly, there must have been some loophole they used to get round this. Sadly, after this was done, the remains of the car were scrapped.

A RALLY-DRIVING JAVELIN OWNER

I am very interested in your article on Jowett cars in this month's issue of the *Dalesman.*

My late husband, Norman Granger, had two Javelins in succession, and I am sure he would have stuck with Jowett cars had they continued in manufacture.

He did a little rallying certainly with one of them, possibly both. He was a member of the Yorkshire Sports Car Club and won a silver tankard which I still have; it is inscribed, 'YSCC Scarborough Rally 29/4/1951 – Team Prize – NW Granger'. This memento does not mention the make of his car, but it was one of the Javelins.

The enclosed snapshot was taken at a breakfast stop and may have been taken on this particular rally, but I cannot be sure, but as I said before he took part in several rallies at this time. On the back of the photo he refers to the car as his 'very excellent and last Javelin'.

I remember him telling me how good the suspension was on these cars: a good example of this is the following little anecdote. He often needed to take a packed lunch with him in the course of his work and on one occasion he forgot to finish his cup of tea before driving off down rough country lanes. The mug was in fact sitting on the picnic shelf that he had fastened to the back of the front seat. On his arrival back at the office, there was the mug of tea still sitting on the shelf and not a drop had been spilt!

He often used to mention Tommy Wise, Tommy Wisdom and Cuth Harrison, who were also involved in rallying. [*Yes, Tommy Wise and Cuth Harrison along with Gerald Palmer – the Javelin designer – won their class in the 1949 Monte Carlo Rally. Tommy Wise and Tommy Wisdom also won their class in a Jupiter in the 1950 Le Mans 24-hour race ... NS]*

I came seriously on the scene in late 1951, and soon after that, married life and the responsibilities attendant on bringing up three children really finished his serious competitive driving.

Norman was a very keen and knowledgeable car driver at all times and set his two sons and one daughter and me on the right lines for driving. He would have been so interested in this article of yours. Sadly he died suddenly in December 1988, so I rather feel that I have written this for him to you, though he would have had a lot more to say!

I am so glad you have brought your Jupiter back to Yorkshire. The photo of you with it at Sandsend brings back memories for me; we had family holidays there for several years.

Mrs Diana Granger ... Thorpe Arch, Wetherby, September 1990

I wrote again to Mrs Granger and had another reply from her:

Yes my father bought his cars from the Jowett agents North Riding Motors of York, which was run by the Shaw family. We also knew them from our mutual interest in playing tennis. I am sorry but I cannot remember the registration of the first Javelin, but I am sure it was EVY***.

One other item of possible interest to you was when we went on honeymoon to France in April 1952 there was a restriction on the amount of money we were allowed to take out of the country. The war was only recently over and rationing was still in place; I think the amount we could take was £25. Due to this my husband had a larger petrol tank fitted into the boot of the Javelin to save having to spend so much of our precious Francs on their petrol!

Diana Granger ... Thorpe Arch, Wetherby, October 1990

R. F. ELLISON – JOWETT GARAGE OWNER

I recently read your book on the history of Jowett Cars Limited; the parts of particular interest to me were the 'Monte' exploits by various Jowett owners.

As a very young teenager in the early fifties, living in Lancashire, I was acquainted with the garage of R. F. Ellison, who was our local Jowett agent. I can still well remember the Javelins and occasional Jupiter gracing the forecourt with their beautiful flowing lines. I seem to remember that most of the Javelins were black, with some others in a pale gold metallic finish.

With my father also in the motor trade, I was kept informed of Bob Ellison's rallying exploits, and remember the arrival of his Jowett 'special', shown on page 106 of your book. This was not, in my eyes, an attractive car, being very slab-sided, and appeared to have a Jupiter grille rather incongruously grafted onto the front.

I was aware that he had come to grief in the 'Monte' but was not aware that the car had, in fact, been recovered and eventually finished the course. Bob Ellison

Robert Ellison with his own Javelin in his workshops prior to the 1949 Monte Carlo Rally, together with his co-driver Walter Mason, a local solicitor. (Ellison)

Robert Ellison's Javelin registered JTJ300 prior to the 1950 Monte Carlo Rally; he is pictured here with his co-driver Walter Mason. This picture was used in the local paper prior to them setting off to Glasgow. (Ellison)

duly returned home apparently unscathed, but I don't ever recall seeing the car again – was it abandoned on the continent? [*The car returned back to the UK and is still alive and well today … NS*]

After Jowetts' demise R. F. Ellison became a Rootes agent, displaying, amongst others of the marque, the stunning Sunbeam Alpine sports cars, but I'm not sure if he continued rallying.

I remember Bob Ellison as a very quiet, very short, stocky little man, renowned for his rather large, floppy beret. The only time I ever spoke to him was some time after he had retired. He told me that he still owned a couple of Javelins, so he had obviously never lost his love of the marque.

I have enclosed some photographs of the garage he commissioned in St Annes back in 1939, designed very much in the style of the thirties, with living accommodation on the first floor. The premises are still used as a garage but, sadly, they are beginning to look a little run down now. The large awning to the left of the workshop entrance is a more recent addition, an extension to a modern car showroom next door.

Keith Hutchinson … Lytham-St-Annes, Lancashire, January 2001

p.s. I'm curious to know why the R1 Jupiter registered HAK364 acquired a different front end treatment during its short life?

The R1 first appeared at the 1951 Le Mans as a sole car registered HAK364; the other two Jupiters in the team that year were standard-bodied cars. Sadly, the R1 retired and one of the standard Jupiters driven by Marcel Becquart and Gordon Wilkins went on to take the 1½-litre class prize. The following year, a team of three R1s were entered. In the 1951 race, it was permitted to have separate 'motorcycle-type' mudguards fitted, but the 1952 regulations stipulated that the wings had to be an integral part of the car, so the front end had to be modified to comply with this regulation.

MORE MEMORIES OF BOB ELLISON

I had been in correspondence with Tony Ellison, Bob's son, in Australia, as he sent me several photographs of his father in the 1951 Monte Carlo Rally. I asked him for any memories he may have of his father. Needless to say, I was delighted with his reply, which I publish here:

Thank you for the text from your new book, *Sporting Jowetts*. I was particularly interested in the final article on my Dad's return to Lytham St Annes, escorted by members of the Lytham St Annes and District Motor Club. It actually gave me a date for the Civic Reception photos! It was a thriving club in those days to produce thirty cars!! I vaguely remember him arriving home, but I don't recall what car he was driving which broke down.

Funnily enough the club was resurrected in the early '60s, and I was a member for a short time, and drove a hotted up Hillman Imp! We were Rootes dealers in those days, up to 1970.

With regard the name Xanthippe, the dictionary says it's the wife of Socrates: the prototype of the quarrelsome, nagging wife. I don't know if that related to an unreliable car!

One of the things I can remember when I was an apprentice (1961-64) motor mechanic, working for my Dad, was having to wash Javelin engine parts. Even then (we were Rootes Dealers in those days) we were still servicing Jowetts, and remember he did do a lot of engine rebuilds, as we had all the kit in the workshop (boring bars, reamers, lathe etc.). He'd needed all that equipment when he ran the garage through the war years.

With regard to my memories of my Dad, I will give you a quick potted history, to set the scene! My Dad was a motor engineer of the first order; he was not a salesman, which in some ways was a disadvantage. However, he took a very personal interest in all the repairs carried out in the garage, and personally road tested every car in for service.

My Mum left him for another man when I was very young, but he spent a lot of time, and money I suppose, in getting custody of me. This would have been around 1948, so I was around when he entered the various rallies, ie, RAC, Tulip, Alpine, and of course the Monte Carlo Rallies. I remember him coming into my bedroom when he arrived back after the 1951 Monte, to tell me he had got back. I was too tired for it to mean anything I suppose then.

I was brought up in a 'Francophile' environment, with all the trips to France etc. that he did, bringing back small presents from his trips. His 'Basque' beret became his trademark, which everyone recognised.

When I became older, he was anxious to take me 'on the continent' to visit all the places he had been. The first time I went to France was in the summer school holidays in 1957; we sailed from Newhaven to Dieppe. That was also the first time he took me to Monte Carlo, which for a thirteen-year-old was quite an experience, I can tell you! Over the next few school summer holidays, we always made the trip across the channel, visiting France, Italy, Germany, Andorra etc. This all came to an end when I left school, and started my apprenticeship with my Dad. Although we did do a couple of trips in later years.

I remember on these trips, he always took the opportunity to buy a new beret to replace the worn one!

It was these trips that gave me the taste for travel, and I have been fortunate over the years to have visited many countries.

He encouraged me to join Round Table, as he had been in it when he was younger. In fact he was Table Chairman in 1944, the year I was born. I was to become the first 'second generation Chairman' in our Table. I was in Lytham St Annes Round Table, as had been my Dad.

It must have been quite an emotional time for him in 1980, when the garage business went into liquidation. However, it all worked out OK in the end. I went off to Saudi Arabia for fifteen years to do my own thing. It's just a shame we didn't have the information technology we have now, then, as I could have helped my Dad research his history. There are a lot of things I would have loved to have told him, but couldn't if you know what I mean.

Tony Ellison ... Australia, May 2010

A young Ellison at the wheel of a 1920s Short-2. It is interesting to see that it has Xanthippe written on the side of the bonnet. I asked his son Tony if he knew what the significance was behind the name. He did not know for sure, but the dictionary says it's the wife of Socrates; the prototype of the quarrelsome, nagging wife. I don't know if that related to an unreliable car!

A youthful Tony Ellison with his father at the official St Annes-on-Sea Civic welcome home celebrations after the class win in the 1951 Monte Carlo Rally. (Ellison)

Robert Ellison had a special-bodied Jupiter built for him by J. E. Farr & Son of Blackburn to use in the 1952 Monte Carlo Rally, one of four they built. He encountered heavy snow in the Saint-Flour area 130 miles from Nevers, sliding off the road into a ravine thirty feet below. The following day the car was dragged back onto the road by a team of oxen. The car was badly damaged, but amazingly it was able to reach Monte Carlo, but was not an official finisher, as it was a day late. (Ellison)

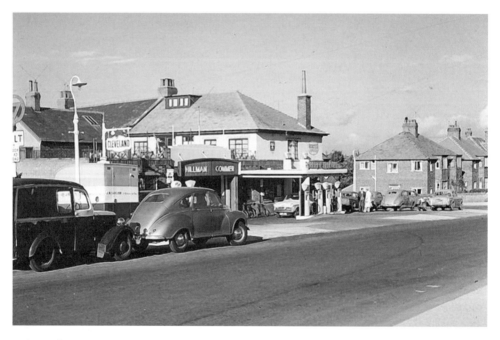

Robert Ellison's garage in St Annes-on-Sea taken in the early 1960s. By this time, they had switched to a Roots dealership, but still maintained Jowetts, as can be evidenced by the two Javelins and a Bradford in the picture. (Ellison)

MEMORIES OF PRE-WAR JOWETT OWNERS

THE JOYS OF JOWETTEERING

I suppose it all started late in the winter of 1946/47 when the worst of the snow receded. I was working as a bus conductor on a double-decker in the Halifax area, on a regular route and with a regular driver. He asked me quite bluntly one day, during lay-over time at our out of town terminus, 'Does tha drive?' to which I replied in the negative. He countered this by saying, 'Get thissen in't tha cab and I will show thee.' As the bus in question was a 1931 Leyland Titan I needed no second bidding. This had to be heaven of the very best kind! He then explained the gear positions and the necessity for double de-clutching which I sampled. After this he initiated me into the starting of this dear old lady – she was fitted with an 8.6 litre diesel engine – which had a lovely purr.

After all this, it was time to depart but he often let me drive her along to the first stop, and on occasions, let me reverse it back into the terminus. Then on quiet Saturday mornings and on Easter and Whit Monday and Tuesday mornings he would let me drive her the last two miles to the terminus.

Now this is where the Jowett enters the stage, to become something of a star in a way. Sometime in 1955 a cousin of mine, who lived in Idle, and worked at Jowett Cars, bought a 1931 Jowett which I have since heard referred to as a Flying Fox. Be that as it may, my cousin always referred to her as 'The Old Lady.' She eventually came to us for the princely sum of £12, so I obtained my first provisional licence. After driving the Titan unofficially for so long, I had to get used to the different pedal layout and gearbox positions, and until the Suez crisis I was always accompanied. During the crisis however it was possible to drive a car unaccompanied as a provisional driver; needless to say I took full advantage of this!

Until we were able to obtain a garage for her, KW3897 had to sleep outside, and on the occasion she was to be moved into her new home she steadfastly refused to start. So we had to resort to the 'magic wand' and swung the starting handle over and over again. The names we called that inoffensive car had to be heard to be believed. In my younger days I learned many swear words at Sunday

THE
"1928"
JOWETT

"For now he's free to sing and play, over the hills and far away"

R.C. Stevenson

"We are seven."

school, but my friend Beau taught me some more that day! After some twenty minutes or so I suggested we stopped for a cigarette break and put my hand in my pocket for my lighter. It was there, but so was the rotor arm that I had taken off it the night before to secure it. This caused a second wave of swearing from Beau, which lasted for some considerable time! He now said that the car was a little sweetheart, but he never forgave me for that short lapse in memory.

On one occasion we were out with a friend accompanying me; he was a bus driver and I don't think that he had ever crossed swords with a Jowett before. I thought it would be fun to lay a trap for him, and it happened thus – the evening was dark and we were on a badly lit road, and I asked if he would care to drive for a while. We changed places whereupon he selected what he thought was first gear and attempted to move off. Blind panic set in when we shot off in reverse; I shone my torch down onto the pedals and showed him the gear positions. He was shocked to see only three forward gears, to which I said, 'How many more do you want.' After stalling the car twice, he moved back into the passenger seat, saying 'enough is enough', vowing he would never sit in the driving seat again! He also made me promise not to say anything about it to the lads at work, as he wanted to preserve his dignity.

One Sunday afternoon we set off from home, full of confidence and the joys of spring, and 200 yards down the road we came to a rapid halt, when a steering coupling broke. We managed to obtain the required parts locally and my brother affected the necessary repairs. The afternoon drive was now abandoned but, ever dauntless, we sallied forth in the evening to visit local hostelries, one of which was at Fartown. On leaving, and just passing the rugby ground, I saw a torch ahead being waved at me; I recognised the owner as our local police sergeant. Realisation dawned, I had set off without any lights on, as I pulled up I put my side-lights on and pulled my licence out of my breast pocket. As I handed it over I said, 'That was damn stupid of me, wasn't it sergeant?' He said, 'It was indeed,' and put his torch on my licence, and after noting the issue date handed it back to me saying, 'Good night sir and have a good journey!'

Now the following summer we ventured forth one afternoon to sample some country scenery, and after a stop for tea and scones I decided to climb a nearby hill to gain access to some particularly pleasant countryside with which I had become familiar as a cyclist when younger and single. I may be wrong in saying this, but I am sure it was 1 in 4 at its steepest, but it certainly made the old lady gasp a bit, she was however shaking rather badly, but over the top she went, valiantly. I was alarmed to think that I may have done her some harm, so I switched her off, climbed out and opened the bonnet to have a look, even though I did not have a clue as to what I was looking for. The cause however was obvious even to me; one of the plug leads was off! It was the spade-type held in place by a small nut, this was clearly in the road somewhere, but I managed to find a similar-sized one to make the repair. The fact remains that this game old lady had come over the top of this 1 in 4 hill on one cylinder with two overfed adults on her back.

My cousin always claimed that provided there was something to grab hold of, a Jowett would climb a vertical house end and when, later, I told him about what she had done; he was not in the least bit surprised. His main reaction was to say, 'Jowetts are the best things on wheels.' He believed wholeheartedly in Jowett cars and it must have rubbed off on me. However, knowing the area somewhat, I tried her for starting, and she coughed and fired up and though still shaking but not so badly, I took her by a shorter downhill route to the Sovereign at Shepley Top and then across the road to the garage, where I summoned help. The mechanic looked at her and opened the bonnet, and I showed him the trouble.

'How far have you come like this?' he asked. I said, 'From Syke Bottom over the top to Piper Wells and down here to you off the Birdsedge Road.' He went on to say, 'I allus knew these could go anywhere,' and went to fetch a nut and spanner. In a trice she was ready to go again, and I asked him how much he wanted. 'Put that down to experience,' he said, 'I just wish that car were mine!' In 1957 he was clearly a few years ahead of the restoration scene which would start to take off in the mid-1960s.

So the lovely little Jowett gave us no further trouble for as long as we had her, but we were offered a newer car, an Austin 18 of 1935, so we traded in KW3897 and proudly drove off in the Austin.

A sequel to this saga concerns my cousin again, when we acquired KW3897, he in turn acquired a Bradford van registered MPC450, which had two side windows fitted at some time. There came a time that he and his wife were returning home from a trip to Kent, and somewhere in the region of Hatfield the crankshaft broke. So they had to park it up and returned home to Bradford on the train. The following weekend he returned to collect it with the aid of two friends. Having got back to base, so to speak, there was a discussion about a replacement engine. The next part of the story I am sure you will not want to read, but the outcome of this was the fitting, with perfectly made mouldings, a Vauxhall 10 engine and the van forthwith ran beautifully.

The following summer of 1962, he lent me the van for my fortnight holiday, as we were 'wheel-less' at the time (I should have kept the Jowett!). We set off for the day halfway through the first week, and by this time we were driving in the Queensbury area. I stopped on the way down to Odsal Top to fill up with petrol and asked for half a pint of oil. You could still buy it from a tank by filling an oil can up with it. When the petrol attendant came with the can of oil, he told me I had opened the wrong side of the bonnet. 'No I haven't I said', 'Yes you have' he said. He then had a look under the bonnet and said, 'What the 'ells that then?' 'An engine,' I said, to which he said, 'Very droll,' before taking a closer look. 'A Vauxhall.' he said incredulously. 'And some lovely mountings too; that's no shoddy job – did you do it?' 'No,' I said. 'It was done by my cousin and two of his friends, who were in the motor trade.' So I then went on to tell him the story of what they did.

So after that fortnight was over and MPC450 was returned to Idle, I never got the chance to drive it again or any other Jowett for that matter.

Ken Butler ... Whitby 1988

MEMORIES OF EVA

This article was taken from issue number 86 of Yorkshire's nostalgic magazine Down Your Way. *It was also reproduced in the November 2006* Jowetteer.

I think everyone will remember their first car. Mine was a Jowett registered EV7073, which was a circa 1931 model. It had a maroon body with a black boot, and running boards along either side in true 'gangster' fashion. These were so wide that, had it been driven in India for example, they would have accommodated eight extra passengers – maybe more! At the time I was twenty-five years old and working in London. My boyfriend had heard of a colleague who was anxious to sell his car at a knock-down price and he (my boyfriend) inveigled me into raiding my bank account to the tune of £40. Not such a knock-down price in 1953 and almost a fifth of my entire wealth. At the time I had no driving licence, but Tom had, so I succumbed. I knew nothing about cars and I had no wish to know, but circumstances soon prompted me to learn all about *Eva*'s little quirks – and there were plenty.

First off, the dynamo didn't work properly, which meant that from time to time we had to give the old girl a rest until she had generated enough spark to continue on her laborious way. Secondly, the battery was decidedly temperamental; a combination of defects provided us with some hilarious and scary moments. It could be said that *Eva* was the forerunner of the present day 'stretch' limousine, although 'runner' may not be entirely appropriate. She was more of an 'ambler', but stretch she did. The distance between the front and rear seats made normal conversation with anyone misguided enough to travel with us a virtual shouting match. It was this elongated seating arrangement that was to play a part in one of our more bizarre experiences. We had been out dancing at the Locarno Ballroom in Streatham on a bitterly cold and foggy November evening; I was dolled up to the nines in my old fur coat, the sleeves of which finished where a pair of very unstylish yellow woolly gloves began. The first worrying sound I heard was a loud knocking from somewhere beneath my feet.

'The big end's gone,' said Tom laconically; he didn't seem too concerned, and so I returned to my pastime of watching the world go by from the comfort of our newly acquired chariot. But not for long; suddenly all the lights on the car shut down; this time Tom seemed less unconcerned.

'The battery lead's broken from the chassis,' he said, trying not to display too much urgency. He may as well have spoken in Chinese for all it meant to me. He stopped the car, pushed back his seat, and started to remove part of the floor. I thought he was dismantling the car in disgust, but suddenly – lo and behold – nestling between his feet was the offending piece of equipment and swinging from one corner enjoying its new-found freedom was the miscreant. 'You will have to hold this lead in place until we get home' instructed Tom with some authority. I looked at him in amazement. 'How on earth do I do that?' I asked. After all, I was hardly dressed for a mechanical job. Tom looked at me with barely concealed impatience. 'You lean down and put your arm through the floor, naturally.' 'Oh naturally,' I said sarcastically. The thought of a force ten gale blowing up my coat sleeve for two or three miles did not appeal. After showing me where the lead had to go, he said rather brusquely, 'Come on then!' at which I started to lower myself to the floor and gingerly completed the hand-over.

'What are you going to be doing?' I asked through the hole in the floor. 'Driving of course,' he replied. 'From here if I can.' 'Here' was practically on the back seat, the idea being to give me as much room as possible in which to perform my acrobatics. It was a good job he was six feet tall and had exceptionally long arms; otherwise it would have been a complete impossibility. And so we set off. I had two real concerns; one that I would get a thump in my ear from a hefty size nine, and secondly, that my hand would become so numb with the cold that I would drop the lead from the anchorage. Tom was leaning backwards at full stretch peering through the bottom of the steering wheel. It was hilarious and a state of giggling threatened to overwhelm me but I thought that Tom, with his concentration in overdrive, would not appreciate the funny side of the situation. Suddenly I heard him chuckle. With relief I joined in, but it was not our predicament which had prompted the hilarity, as he told me later. It was the sight of a group of people standing at a bus stop turning as one, mouths agape on seeing an apparently driverless car cruising past them in the fog. Their horror-filled faces amused Tom so much we had to stop and re-group before continuing on our way.

Tom and I married some two years later and we often laugh at that frenzied journey. *Eva* went for scrap in the early 1960s for the princely sum of £3. If we had kept her, she may have made our fortune as a collector's item. She was an elegant old girl and great fun. Al Capone would have been proud to have her in his fleet.

> *I wonder if he would have been, as she would not have had a great turn of speed as a getaway car! Following the 'Memories of Eva' article, I wrote to the editor of the* Down Your Way *magazine, asking if my letter addressed to Mrs Watson could be forwarded on to her on my behalf; this they must duly have done, as I received this lovely note from her:*

I was so pleased to receive your letter dated 9 July, which arrived yesterday. It seems to have taken a while to get to me; nevertheless, I am grateful to Averil for forwarding it on to me. I am glad you enjoyed the article but I'm so sorry I have no reasonable photos to send to you. I wish I had, but I was not into photography at the time. I have had many cars over the years since dear old Eva, but none with the same character. I remember Tom, my husband, and I never said 'the car' it was always 'Eva', like one of the family, albeit sometimes a troublesome one.

I recall another incident when the dynamo needed rewinding and I trudged from Edgeware to Burnt Oak on the outskirts of London to find a garage that could do the job with this seemingly ton weight in the bottom of my shopping bag. (Happy days!)

I do hope you may be able to publish a second selection of *My Car was a Jowett*. If you do, let me know, as I would like to buy a copy.

Irene M. Watson … Sutton, Hull, July 2005

PRE-WAR JOWETT VAN JOTTINGS

I worked at Jackson's Garage in Kendal from the age of fourteen, and after the first year I was the only mechanic there, as this was at the beginning of the war and the other mechanics were called-up. I was working with my boss and his wife, who did all the office work. During the war we had to work on many different types of transport, including cars, vans, lorries, tractors, stationary engines etc. I worked a 5½ day week, which always included a full day on Saturday, my wage for the first year was 10 shillings (50p) a week. I also delivered the newspapers from the local Post Office from 7 a.m. – 8.30 a.m. prior to starting work at the garage; for this I received 15 shillings (75p) per week. By the time I left the motor trade in 1956, I was head mechanic and paid £9 17s 6d, plus an extra £5 if I worked the full weekend.

In 1951, when talking to a fellow motorcyclist, who was one of the four mechanics at H. J. Croft in the main street of Kendal, who were agents for Morris and Rover cars, he told me that they worked a five day week, Monday to Friday, and every fifth weekend for which they were paid £5 10 shillings. So I moved from Jackson's Garage to Croft's and then found out that each mechanic had an apprentice to work with them, even when doing the whole weekend extra.

At an early part of the time I was working for Croft's, a new workshop was built at the top of the slope that led into a large yard behind the garage where quite a few vehicles were often parked.

One of the vehicles that had been parked there for some time was a 1930s Jowett van that was owned by a Mr Dodd. When he came in for petrol I asked him what he was going to do with it, and he said he planned to sell it shortly. At a slightly later date, cash changed hands, and I was now the proud owner of the Jowett van registered JM4802.

As Mr Croft allowed us to work on our own vehicles at night in the garage, providing we were not doing work on other people's cars, I spent quite some time working on the van to make it in good condition, so I could use it every day.

As the front shock absorbers were not very good, one of my first jobs on the van was to fit new modern ones to the front. This meant that I had to make and fit large metal plates to the chassis to be able to bolt the tops of the shock absorbers to it. Another job I did was fitting a two-way switch to the steering column; one side of it worked the interior light, and the other side of the switch worked the 'flame-thrower' spot lamp that I fitted to the front of the van. These spot lamps were known as 'flame-throwers' because if you stopped very close to the car in front of you when it was switched on, it would blister the paintwork of the car in front of you!

Rushing to fit the spot lamp, one night when I was working in the garage, I managed to drill a hole into the radiator, so I had to remove it, and take it to the upstairs workshop to repair it – It was a very late supper for me that night!

A visit to Murphy's Scrapyard in Kendal produced a large bench seat with a back fitted to it, which, I had been told, came out of an old American car, and it was a very good fit inside the rear of the van. After a coat of blue paint to try and cover up the lettering on the sides of the van, it was ready for the road, as there were no MOTs in those days!

One of my fellow mechanics at Croft's was Jack, who had a 1934 Austin 7 tourer, and we decided to visit the road racing at Scarborough. In those days there used to be a crowd at the top of Sutton Bank watching cars making the ascent. When Jack's Austin 7 and my old Jowett reached the top, there was a loud cheer from the crowd.

Quite a lot of the villages around Kendal used to have village hall dances on Friday nights; there were also some dances at the Church Hall in Kendal. On these nights we would have a few drinks before going into the dance, we would park the Jowett in the car park with the doors unlocked, giving access to the large bench seat in the rear! That Jowett was well known to the local girls and most of them always refused any offers of a ride in the van, although they were still keen to accept a lift on any of our motorcycles.

During the war we had an evacuee from the North East staying at my parent's house, and at the end of the war he stayed on in Kendal, and at a later date, he worked at the County Hall, and from there he joined the Navy. He also married a local girl, and after the wedding, everyone went to the bride's parents' house, who lived on the Kirkbarrow Estate. As the main railway line at Oxenholme was 2 miles from Kendal, the happy couple had a taxi to take them there so they could set off on their honeymoon. As they drove off, I shouted out that I was going to the station to see them off, and if any of the guests wanted to come, they should jump in the Jowett. Part of the road to the station was slightly uphill, and the Jowett did not seem to be pulling very well, and I thought I would have to look at the engine the following day. This was not necessary, as I realised when I reached the station there were no less than twelve people inside! I was lucky, as most of them were women and children, or I could have been fitting new rear springs.

One of the passengers was an old lady, who had clearly bought a new powder-blue outfit for the wedding, with matching hat. She must have been sitting on somebody's knee in the back of the van, as her head had been hitting the roof of the van, as her outfit was covered in muck that had come out of the padded canvas roof. She was now not very pleased at all, as her hat and outfit were looking very grubby.

I think it was because I owned a Jowett at the time, our foreman at Croft's told me to leave the job I was doing and work on a Jowett car that had just come into the workshop; the driver was complaining about lack of power on the Lakeland Hills. As I had, during one of my weekend stints, a Jaguar from the South of England with the same complaint, I took the front wheels off the Jowett and checked the plugs. As with the Jaguar, it had been fitted with the wrong plugs, so I fitted the correct ones. After checking the ignition and the carburettor, I was told the driver paid the bill and set off like a bat out of hell down Kendal High Street. In those days, one of the starting points for the Monte Carlo Rally was Glasgow, and this Jowett was one of the entries. I cannot be sure, but I think the car was a Javelin, but it could have been a Jupiter – it is a long time ago! [*I am almost sure this will have been a Javelin, as the driver sounded as if he were a private entrant; also, I am sure Brian would not have taken the front wheels off a Jupiter to change the plugs ... NS*]

I have owned forty-one motorcycles, thirty-five cars, seven vans, four pick-ups, and a three-wheeled Morgan that was fitted with a 1000cc V Twin engine. Some of these have stuck in my mind as being value for money; the Jowett van was one of them. I sold the Morgan for £160 in 1951; what would it be worth now? I will have to stop writing this now and mop up the tears!

Brian Shepherd ... Kendal, 2008

In this account, Brian does not say that his old van was in fact a 10-hp four-cylinder Jowett van, a model of which only 201 were built. Sadly, no examples of this model survive, I am going to have to stop writing this now so I can wipe away my tears!

LONG MEMORIES OF JOWETT CARS

I noted your letter in the *Daily Telegraph* of 17 February, and whilst I no longer own a Jowett, alas, I have had a fair bit of experience of the breed over a long lifetime and perhaps these few remarks will be of interest to you.

My first sight of a Jowett car was when I was six years of age – sixty-eight years ago – the vehicle belonged to a Mr Élan who was manager of Martin's Bank in Shipley at the time. He used to park it outside my father's office; it was a two-seater with a dickey seat and a huge brass radiator. I used to climb into the car and pretend to drive it with much 'Vroom vroom-ing' and clutching of the steering wheel.

It had a self-starter and apparently I knew how to use it, as on one epic occasion I invited my unsuspecting mother to join me in the car for a ride. To humour the child she stepped into the car and before she had time to blink it appears that I started the engine and somehow or other managed to get it into gear. And to increasingly high decibel yells of terror from mother set off in a series of jerks along Wharf Street. Father dashed out of his office and stopped the whole thing – between calming his wife and giving me a damn good hiding he had quite a busy few minutes!

Towards the end of the war while I was at home on leave I went to see my brother, who lived at Apperley Bridge, and had to go past the Jowett factory. Several times we saw a strange futuristic-looking car going like a bloody rocket up King's Road (a fairly long straight new road running up to Five Lane Ends in Idle). The strange vehicle turned out to be the Javelin on test runs shortly before being unveiled at the Bradford Exhibition shortly after the end of the war.

In the early Fifties my father asked my advice about the purchase of a new car to replace his aging Vauxhall and rather to my surprise he asked, 'What do you reckon to these Javelins?' I found a garage dealing in the cars and arranged a test drive for him, but I went on the trip as well. The owner of the garage, with whom I had a slight acquaintance, did the demo himself, and nearly frightened my father out of his wits. Arriving back at the garage we did a swift figure of eight around the petrol pumps and I, sitting in the back of the car thought 'You've blown it' but to my surprise father bought the car which was a year old at the time and ran it for a good number of years. It was a joy to drive; my first experience of driving a new Javelin was memorable, in fact, I have rarely felt such a thrill in a car as I did in that one.

Once I had got used to the pedals, being slightly to the left of normal, it seemed to be the most exciting thing I had ever handled, and in subsequent drives in father's car I never lost that pleasurable feeling. Totally with you; never for a moment did I feel that the car would not respond to what ever it was asked to do. The beautiful wheel-mounted gear lever was a joy to use – so positive and accurate. Around the same period I drove a Triumph Roadster which had a similarly mounted gear lever and it felt like changing gear with springy wires as controls. The Javelin box and controls were marvellous in comparison.

In the early '50s I had a new Bradford 'shooting brake' as my personal car and ran it for several years. On one occasion when driving the car up a hill from Kirkstall to Horsforth I heard a very loud bang under the bonnet and the car immediately began to shake violently. Pulling into the side of the road I switched the engine off (as it was still running at that stage) and opened the bonnet. The left-hand cylinder had snapped off near the crankcase, because the piston for some reason had seized in the bore and on its outward travel had exerted such force that the whole contraption snapped off. So for the few moments as I pulled off the road and switched off the ignition the cylinder block complete had been going in and out at the end of the piston rod, driven by the right-hand side that was still operating normally. Horsforth Garage replaced the left piston block and the whole of the left-hand assembly and I had the car back again the next day and never had a minute's trouble with it again. In the Bradford I toured the UK, always enjoying the driving, and it never let me down again in any way.

As a small boy I remember somebody talking about a vintage Jowett saying, 'They don't go very fast but they'll pull you up a bloody house side.' This was certainly true of the Bradford as well.

In the 1960s I bought a rather clapped-out Javelin for my daughter who had just passed her test. I remember one humorous occasion when she went to collect her small brothers and a few more little boys from a party. It was dark, and having driven to the house perfectly well and the car behaving correctly she loaded a fair number of little boys into the back of the car and, presto – no lights would light up and the engine would not start – zero electrics. They all climbed out and the lights came back on again at full brightness, so they all climbed back into the car again and the lights all went out again! This happened several times until they realised the weight of the boys was pressing the springs of the rear seat across the battery terminals and, of course, shorted everything out. This was because the insulation board was missing; but eventually the poor child arrived with her cargo of little boys, some in the front and the rest standing up in the back of the car leaning over the front seat to keep as much weight as possible off the back seat and floor. It was not a problem to rectify but one can imagine the thoughts of a young girl and her little cargo of small hellions when as though by magic the lights went on and off.

I don't know if the above is of interest – probably not, so throw it away! [*This is too good to throw away Geoffrey! … NS*]

Geoffrey Rennard … Alderney, Channel Islands, March 1996

A BARCLAYS BANK PENSIONER'S PRE-WAR JOWETT MEMORiES

I have just read your article in the *Barclays News* about your Jowett Jupiter; I found this most interesting as I drove Jowetts many years ago. It all started in 1922 when I read an article in the *Autocar* about the performance of the Jowett in the Scottish Six Days Trial. As a schoolboy I was hooked on them and in 1928 I managed to persuade my father to buy one. This was a 7-hp saloon with two doors, both on the nearside. So you had a gate change gearbox on your right; as my father did not drive, I had sole use of the car.

We kept this car until 1932, when I managed to get my father to buy a new one; this one had four doors. We kept this car until early into the war, when I sold it to a friend who needed a car to get to work on a cross-country route. I can still remember this transaction, as we had to buy some petrol and there was a lot of shrapnel coming down at the time.

In those days the annual tax was only £7 and I can remember buying Russian petrol for it (R.O.P) for 10 old pence a gallon, which is about 4p in new money.

Failing eye sight has at last caught up with me and I am having to sell my present car (a Ford Fiesta) and give up driving altogether. The traffic round here is not like what it was sixty years ago!

I seem to remember that back in 1922 the price of a Jowett two-seater (the only model made) was about £170 and if you had an electric starter fitted it was £10 extra. Our 1928 model had an electric starter but even so you often had to start it by hand. I can still well remember many a bruised and bloody knuckle when the engine back fired and the handle kicked back! We didn't have a windscreen wiper and a tip for a rainy day was to cut a potato in half and smear it across the glass. Skids were also very common, especially on tram lines, as the tyres would get stuck in them. I remember a friend of mine with a Citroën Clover Leaf guiding himself in the fog (a real London Pea-Souper) by following the tram lines. This worked really well for a while until he found himself at the tram depot!

After the war I had a demonstration run in a Javelin, in the course of which we ran out of petrol. Whether this put me off I cannot recall, but I did not buy one; I got a Ford Anglia instead.

On a personal note, I retired from Barclays Wimbledon Common branch in 1968, where I was a manager's assistant.

I wrote back to Brian and had this entertaining reply from him:

You ask about the registration numbers of my two Jowetts. I am pretty sure that the first one was YW6077 but I cannot guarantee this, my father bought it new from Normands Garage in Hammersmith for about £170. It had a maroon fabric body with a top speed on the level of 43 mph.

The second car was bought from AV Motors, Teddington; if you ever went to the Barclays Training Centre in Teddington, the garage was just across the road from the railway station next to the Clarendon Hotel; it is now a block of offices. The registration number of this one was MV6912; it had a sliding roof and a top speed on the flat of 47 mph – how things have changed since I started motoring in 1928.

I can recall going to Whitby in the 1950s and called into Barclays Bank to cash a cheque. This was when the railway came into Whitby after crossing the high trestle viaduct at Sandsend.

Brian Wood ... Twickenham, March 1991

Brian made several references to Barclays Bank in his letters. This was because my request for Jowett information had been published in Barclays' in-house staff magazine. In a previous life I worked for Barclays bank for just over thirty years at branches in York, Selby, Whitby and Scarborough. It was Brian's ambition to be able to draw his Barclays pension for longer than his working life with them. I am very pleased to say he managed this some time ago, as he is still going strong (2010). I have now been drawing mine for ten years, so only another twenty to go!

MEMORIES OF A TOUR OF SCOTLAND IN A 1934 7-HP JOWETT SALOON

The 1934 Jowett registered JB4691 was my first car, and I was very proud of it, I was confident it was capable of making a trip round Scotland which was something I always wanted to do, so I planned the route accordingly. It was in June 1951 when we set out in the Jowett; it was coloured black and green, so we thought it would blend in with the countryside!

Living in Surrey at the time, it was going to be a long haul to the Border, 329 miles to Gretna if my memory is correct. I had calculated with stops that the average speed would be about 20 mph, which proved about right. Armed with a route map from the AA, we set off at 6 a.m. and proceeded in a north westerly direction through the Midlands reaching Warrington and then headed North to pass through the towns of Wigan and Preston, arriving at the town of Lancaster by the early evening. Deciding that this was enough travelling for one day, we quickly found accommodation for the night.

Day two (Sunday) was via the Lake District, which we all know to be a very scenic area through which we did not wish to rush. Being a warm day and with long climbs the needle in the thermometer frequently went to the boil position, thus necessitating stops to allow the engine to cool. By late afternoon we had passed through Carlisle and to the Border at Gretna Green, where the blacksmith's shop was viewed. We were then on the A74, the main artery for traffic from Carlisle to Glasgow, which in those days was an average single-carriageway road. We reached Lockerbie by the evening so we decided to 'call it a day'; the Blue Bell Hotel was a very nice place to stay.

Leaving Lockerbie on Monday morning we headed north through very pleasant Southern Uplands towards Glasgow. Again the weather was warm and sunny and the distinctive sound of the twin-cylinder engine as we cruised along was music to our ears. Skirting the south west of Glasgow in accordance with the AA instructions, somehow an error was made which resulted in becoming more involved with the outskirts of Glasgow than we had hoped for. I cannot remember now where the Clyde was crossed, but eventually we found ourselves on the Great Western Road heading for Loch Lomond. That day, the song description 'the bonny banks of Loch Lomond' was certainly true. It was a lovely drive, with the road winding along the western side, with blue water on the right, and on the left, wooded areas with colourful rhododendrons in places.

At Tarbet the right fork was taken and the course set for Crianalarich; this stretch of road ran parallel with the railway and was little used by motorised traffic, as grass was growing in the middle of the road. Continuing alongside the water past Loch Sloy power station through wooded and undulating scenery, the northern end of Loch Lomond came into view, which was the start of a long and steady climb through Loch Falloch. By now it was late afternoon and the car was suffering with overheating. Descending into the village of Crianalarich one had a feeling of remoteness coupled with the sense of adventure. Soon afterwards we reached Bridge of Orchy where accommodation was found at the Inverason Hotel. A walk in the evening was thoroughly enjoyed, revelling in the quietness and remoteness of the setting with the Highland scenery and the freshness of the air.

Tuesday found us heading further into wild and remote scenery, beyond Bridge of Orchy the terrain was fairly flat, but that was not for long; soon we started on a steep incline heading for Rannoch Moor, this required engaging second gear for several miles. At this higher altitude the scenery changed to moorland and peat bog. We then came down the Pass of Glencoe to Glencoe village. We then carried on this scenic route towards Fort William, at that time Fort William was a nice little West Highland town very different from what exists now. I remember stopping at a chemists shop in the main street to buy some methylated spirit for the small camping stove we carried. It was then the law in Scotland to sign the poisons book for that commodity.

Moving north from Fort William we continued up the Great Glen alongside Lochs Lochy and Ness, turning west heading for Kyle of Lochalsh. This was a typical single-track highland road with sharp hump-backed bridges. At the start of the road there was a sign which read, 'Heavy road construction for sixteen miles.' Fortunately this did not extend for the whole of the distance, but at intermittent stretches with new surfaces in-between. Nevertheless it was fairly slow going as we pressed on through scenery which varied between pleasant wooded areas and stretches of barren hillside.

We finally reached Kyle of Lochalsh, where we stayed overnight, ready to catch the ferry across to Skye on Wednesday morning. The cost of the ferry was 10s for a single and 16s 11d return for cars up to 12 hp and 15s 8d single and £1 5s return for cars over 12 hp. On this occasion JB4691 was the only car waiting for the ferry that morning. Once on the island it was our intention to reach Portree, but that was not achieved. The roads were so bad it was only wise to travel between 15 and 20 mph. So on reaching Sligachan it was decided to retrace our steps back to the ferry, as we did not want to miss it.

Once back on the mainland we travelled east for about six miles alongside Loch Alsh, then turned north and after a steep ascent and descent we arrived at Stromeferry. This was where we caught another ferry with a capacity to carry two cars, the charge for which was another 10s. Having crossed Loch Carron it was only a short distance to the village of the same name, where the night was spent in its comfortable hotel overlooking the Loch.

Thursday was a shorter day in terms of mileage, the road from Loch Carron to Garve was again a typical single track. We were well up to schedule and the weather was grand, so much time was spent in the sunshine enjoying the views. After Garve there was a pleasant run via Muir of Ord, the Jowett happily cruised into Inverness.

I cannot remember the route taken from Inverness on Friday, but I know it was down the A9 for some distance before turning east and traversing some interesting terrain, reaching Aberdeen in late afternoon. It was then on to Royal Deeside where the stop for the night was made at Aboyne.

On Saturday morning we took the road which runs along the south side of the River Dee from Aboyne to Balmoral, the pleasant wooded valley provided a contrast to the mountain and moorland scenery of recent days. Towards the end of Royal Deeside the road starts to climb and eventually Braemar was reached, about 1,100 feet above sea level. We were now high in the mountains but we continued to climb until we reached the famous Devil's Elbow. Stopping at the top for a while the Jowett eased down the steep and winding descent with frequent application of the brakes. I remember thinking at the time that it was easier to descend than ascend, as one could find oneself in difficulties if first gear could not be located at the right moment. It was then an easy run to the night stop at Pitlochry.

Sunday provided a pleasant amble along the A9 to Perth then off onto minor roads to cross the River Forth by way of the Kincardine Bridge to Edinburgh. There was nothing of particular interest in that area so we motored on to Dunbar. Proceeding in a homeward direction, there was a feeling of anti-climax.

We bade farewell to Scotland on Monday morning and headed south as far as Sunderland for the purpose of visiting friends. We then continued south again the following day and stayed the night at Helmsley, a charming market town in North Yorkshire. We left Helmsley on Wednesday morning, when a problem occurred; the route was up a steep hill at Staxton then along an undulating road towards Driffield. Climbing a sharp incline in bottom gear the clutch started to slip, bringing the car to a standstill. Reversing to a safe position lower down the hill, I turned the car round. As reverse gear was a lower ratio than bottom, I tried to reverse up the hill; this was not successful as the Jowett started to boil and the clutch started to slip again. Naturally we had to find a less adventurous route round.

This problem had occurred once before early in the holiday travelling north near Moffatt, apparently some oil had found its way on to the clutch lining.

take a good look when it passes you

Ian Hill pictured with his 1934 Jowett 7-hp saloon registered JB4691 after his epic trip round Scotland in the autumn of 1951. This picture was taken on the North Yorkshire Moors on his way back from Scotland. (Hill)

In 1955, Ian Hill sold his 1934 Jowett and bought a 1938 four-cylinder 10-hp model registered HMK656, this car was also used on a trip round Scotland with four adults and a dog. He complains that the sun was in the wrong direction when he took the picture as it is reflected off the windscreen – I am delighted he still took the picture! (Hill)

Ian Hill's 1938 10-hp saloon being loaded onto the ferry at Kyle of Lochalsh for the crossing to Stornoway on the Isle of Lewis – no roll-on roll-off ferries in those days! (Hill)

I do not remember anything else of interest on the way back over the last three or four days, which consisted of visiting friends on the route back home. The weather for the whole fortnight had been fine and sunny as well as very warm at times. The only trouble in the 1,800 mile trip had been the slipping clutch on those two occasions.

In those days many hotels offered garage accommodation space for guest's cars, but space was not always available, but of course this is unheard of now.

In the autumn of 1951 I exchanged JB4691 for a 1938 four-cylinder 10-hp Jowett saloon registered HMK656; the enclosed picture was taken when we had a trial run in it to the West Country at Dartmoor, as you can see the sun was in the wrong direction causing a reflection on the windscreen.

We made another trip to Scotland in 1955, this time in HMK656 with four adults and a dog. The snap shows the car being loaded onto the MV *Loch Seaforth* at Kyle of Lochalsh for the crossing to Stornoway on the Isle of Lewis. Two days prior to the crossing two or three of the offside front spring leafs broke; I managed to limp twenty miles to Oban on the remaining leaf. The garage removed the spring and took it to the local blacksmith for repair. Other than this, it was also a trouble-free trip.

Ian Hill ... Acton, Sudbury, Suffolk, April 2001

MEMORIES OF A PRE-WAR VAN REGISTERED AVT646

I was interested to read your letter in *The Countryman* Volume 104 about Jowett cars and vans, and thought you may be interested in my memories.

My father purchased a Jowett van registered AVT646 from the Michelin Tyre Company Ltd in Stoke in 1939. I think it was rated 7 hp and was designed to carry 6 or 8cwt. Michelin were disposing of a number of vehicles that were 'over age' and he had a choice of two Jowetts and some Fords. I do not know what he paid but £12 to £20 was the normal range.

The van was in company livery and was painted bright yellow with a large red circle on one of the back doors across which was written in large white letters STOP, which I think was an indication of the company's tyres' ability to stop. The van was fitted with Michelin tyres which were broader than usual and at a lower pressure, so always appeared flat. The appearance of the old Jowett amused the neighbours and our local garage proprietor, so the STOP was soon removed, but the yellow paintwork lasted well into the war.

There was only one seat, for the driver, which was a wooden box about 15 inches square and 4 inches deep which doubled up as the tool box. On top of this was a 3 inch very hard cushion, so one sat about 7 inches above a perfectly flat level floor, with no foot-well. This seat was moved to the passenger side and father sat on an old leather seat rescued from an earlier Austin 12. Neither seat was secured to the floor, but with safety in mind, a piece of wood was nailed to the floor in front of each seat to prevent it sliding forward. There was no starter motor so we used a starting handle which had a beautifully polished ebony handgrip. After starting the engine, the handle was secured by looping a section of inner tube attached to the chassis which projected forward, round the handgrip.

To start the engine it was first of all necessary to turn on the petrol switch that was positioned above the passenger's feet because the petrol tank was in the engine compartment immediately below the windscreen and fed the carburettor by gravity. The next action in the sequence was to lift the bonnet on the passenger side, pull the accelerator wire and insert a double thickness of straw (we always carried straw in the back) under the throttle stop screw. One sharp pull on the compression stroke and the engine sprang to life, after warming up and starting off the piece of straw would fall away onto the road.

We had not had the van very long when the wiring caught fire and with the position of the petrol tank was of great concern, but the fire was extinguished and the van had to be left to be rewired. Going back to collect the vehicle a few days later father was met by the apprentice who enquired if his van was the one with 'two motor bike engines' because of the horizontal twin cylinders.

There were no locks on the doors or ignition key, the ignition switch was a knob in the centre of the light switch. Wartime regulations required the vehicle to be made safe to prevent its use to the enemy. This was achieved by bolting a chain to the door pillar and attaching the chain to the steering wheel with a padlock. The doors opened backwards not forwards as they do today.

At one point an attempt was made to fit a starter motor, but this used to jam due to damage to the flywheel. When it could not be rocked free it was necessary to unbolt the motor. On one occasion a duster was used to prevent the nuts falling into the flywheel casing. Unfortunately in the rush to return home the starter motor was slung in the back and the engine started on the handle, but the duster was not removed first and jammed things up. This resulted in a very long delay in getting home again that night and the starter was never fitted again.

In the early 1940s my uncle borrowed the van and drove home in it with very little oil in the engine, which did not do the big end much good. The following week we had an important journey to make and the kids went ahead in relays on bicycles buying oil as they went so there would be no delay in topping up the oil when the van caught up! We did this every five miles or so on a journey of 25 miles.

On our return the big end was removed and there were large holes in the shell. Fortunately the Alvis Car Company had been evacuated from Coventry and were making aero engines in the town. An employee took the big end and re-metalled it over the weekend. Putting it back in was a problem as it needed reaming to fit the crankshaft; father did this by scraping the metal away a little at a time with his pen knife until he achieved a reasonable fit. He used a similar technique when the plate of his false teeth was too tight for his gums! On one of these many trial fittings he dropped the back section of the big end into the sump and could not retrieve it. Fortunately it was before school meals and I was home for lunch, and with my smaller hand I was able to fish about in the sump for the lost part.

The next problem we had was breaking valve springs; there were two springs for each valve, one inside the other. In the end we left the valve covers off which reduced the frequency of the breakages, but I do not know why this helped.

Periodically we were allocated a crate of rejected Hotel Pottery which was very thick and came in 10cwt lots, we had to move it all, or nothing, from the factory. To spread the load, several dozen dinner plates weighing in excess of 1cwt were loaded in the space for the passenger's feet, and I sat on top. I am sure we must have been heavily overloaded, but with the oversize tyres we never had any problems.

Long before we were anywhere near old enough to hold a licence we kids were able to drive the 'yellow peril' as she was affectionately known and we eventually took our tests in her – the forerunner of the post-war Jowett Bradford.

Shortly after the war we had two Bradfords in succession and the old girl was pensioned off. I dismantled it, but many times since I wish I had not done so. The wheels and chassis went to make a horse-drawn vehicle, and our friends fell foul of the local Constable pushing it to the wheelwright's yard because one was sitting on a box steering it on the road.

Needless to say we were all very sad when the factory in Bradford ceased production. We made do with all sorts of things during and after the war, but photography was not within our scope so no photographs exist.

Bob Jenkins ... Walton on the Hill, Stafford, December 1999

THE FLYING CAPTAIN IN HIS WEASEL

Jowett Appeal – *Daily Telegraph*, Saturday 17 September 1996 – I read your appeal with great interest and, although I have never owned a Jowett, you will be pleased to hear that at the age of 7, a Jowett was the first car I ever rode in; hence my abiding curiosity in the make.

The year was 1934, and the car, a Jowett Weasel four-seater open tourer, with the flat-twin horizontally opposed engine, it had a brown fabric-covered body. The owner was a good friend of my father's, and a First World War Tank Corps Captain, who was my childhood hero.

The Captain, having been blown up during the war, had lost his left leg and his right arm. He had a cumbersome artificial leg but no artificial right arm, the empty sleeve being tucked into his jacket pocket. Yet in spite of his severe disablement, he handled the old Jowett Weasel brilliantly. He even managed to light his pipe while driving, as he clamped a matchbox under his arm stump, and his good knee jammed against the steering wheel as he navigated unerringly along the then almost deserted country lanes.

As I remember it, the only concession to the normal layout was a hand-operated throttle control fitted to the steering wheel. We went on many happy trips with the Captain, and my lasting impression is of the unique 'putter-putter' exhaust note of the Jowett engine, and its steady and unfailing reliability.

Horizontally opposed engines have always fascinated me, and their history and development has been a long one. I suppose Jowett must have been the first in the field to see the advantages of the excellent dynamic balance of this type of engine. Citroën and Porsche seem to have followed suit with their air-cooled flat-twin and flat-four, so there must be something special about them.

The Javelin and Jupiter were both examples of brilliant new engineering concepts, marred ... dare I say it, by unattractive body-styling. [*You may say it, but I don't agree ... NS*] If they had hired some elegant body-stylists to complement their advanced engineering ideas, I believe Jowett would be still flourishing today. [*Jowett had gone to ERA for a body design, but THAT was unattractive and not a patch on the in-house Jupiter body design done by Reg Korner ... NS*]

James H. Crafer ... Sutton, Surrey, February 1996

ON THE ROAD WITH JOEY JOWETT

Reading your article about the Jowett Car Club in *This England* magazine, it brought back many happy memories of our first family car, that wonderful old Jowett we called 'Our Joey'. Perhaps my recalling the trips our family did in it is not what you are seeking. Yet I cannot resist re-living my youth in an age that has now disappeared.

In 1928 my father bought a brand new Jowett touring car though where he got the money is a mystery as we were not a wealthy family. All six of us, two adults and four children, lived in a two-up two-down terraced house in Edgbaston, Birmingham. No one in that far from prosperous neighbourhood owned a car, so we felt different, a little superior. My father only drove the car on fine weekends, taking his family for picnics in what was then in the 1920s and 1930s an uncrowded countryside. The car was christened 'Our Joey'.

Our father was clever with his hands; one of his projects was to build a tray that would fit under the rear seat. This contained a set of bakelite (the predecessor of plastic) cups, saucers and plates. These, together with that essential English accessory, a teapot, a Primus stove to boil a kettle of water and some sandwiches, allowed us to picnic in style. The majority of our trips took us to the south of Birmingham, but occasionally we would venture as far as Bourton-on-the-Water in the Cotswolds. The image of this unspoilt little town with its little bridges spanning the shallow river has remained vivid in my memory, so much so that I have been pulled back by its beauty more than once. Of course it had fewer visitors back then but what was really unique was that the roads leading to it were unpaved, chalk white in colour. In many cases there was a gate across the road and often local farm boys would earn a penny opening and closing the gates.

I was only three years old in 1928 so I do not remember the really early days. My three sisters who were two, five and ten years older than me have recalled what I have not. My earliest recollection of the Jowett was sitting on my father's lap as he drove along, also being saluted by the Automobile Association road patrols riding their yellow and black motorcycle and sidecar combinations. How hoity toity we felt when receiving the salute! When it came to fill up with petrol I helped my father hand-pump the fuel into a clear glass dome on top of the pump from where it fed by gravity into the car's tank. A few years ago I visited the Brooklands Museum where these AA tricycles and petrol pumps are on display. Every winter the car was garaged in a lock-up shed near our home until spring arrived when I helped my Dad grind the valves using two different grades of caborundum paste and take the car off its blocks. So all was then ready for another year's motoring.

Our journeys were not limited to day trips around Birmingham; my sisters recall that we once visited Scotland, a long journey in those days. But for sheer endurance and load-carrying capability it would take some feat to top the three-week early 1930s tour of Devon and Cornwall that Old Joey accomplished without a hiccup. Each night we struck camp and the following morning folded it up again and reloaded the car and carried on our way. Each afternoon we would have our eyes peeled looking out for the next camp site on our route. How we managed to prepare meals and washing and getting clothes clean is a mystery to me, but somehow we managed it.

Money was tight in those days so Dad made his own tent sewing the canvas on a pedal sewing machine. He waterproofed the flysheet by boiling it in linseed oil. The tent poles came from Birmingham buses (he worked for the Corporation that ran the city's bus service in those days). The poles were located vertically on the entrance/exit platform of the buses, and they weighed a ton! All this equipment, two adults, four children together with our clothes and food were stored on the mudguards and in a trunk at the back of the car and between us kids!

Even our father could not sustain this gypsy life every year, so he found a camp site on a dairy farm just outside Eastbourne, on the Pevensey Road. This became our annual vacation spot for three weeks. A tall dining tent complete with folding table and chairs supplemented the original tent. Next came a toilet tent complete with a wooden seat. Having taken care of the accommodation the next improvement was an oven using asbestos sandwiched between sheets of aluminium. The stove was heated by a painter's blowtorch, the kind that burned paraffin fuel. Normally these had a bend in them so the heat could easily be directed to a vertical surface. Very carefully this bend was straightened so the flame went straight up into the open bottom of the stove. Roast beef was now back on the Sunday menu! One fellow camper was so impressed with our elaborate campsite that he christened it 'The Grand Hotel'. When my two eldest sisters finished school and went to work they had neither the time or desire to camp. This did not save much room in the car or the tents as a large St Bernard dog replaced them. Fortunately for the Jowett, not forgetting our father, all of our camping equipment was stored at the farm at the end of our three-week holiday, making it unnecessary to haul it back and forth each year. We left it behind in August 1939 and our father died in 1942, so sadly, we never returned to The Grand Hotel.

The greatest test of the Jowett came on Mucklow's Hill, a notoriously steep gradient outside Birmingham. While climbing it one afternoon with everyone on board a connecting rod broke on old Joey. What better proof of the rugged strength of the engine than the fact that the car still made it up the hill on just one cylinder?

My sister is almost sure that old Joey's registration number was OX6423, but I can tell you that it was coloured British Racing Green, but Heaven knows he was no speedster!

In about 1938 a Morris 8 replaced the Jowett; this was a saloon so the comfort level increased considerably. In addition, there was a starter button, so there was no need to hand-crank the Morris. As a youth I was all in favour of the greatly improved transportation, particularly its increased power. Yet if granted a wish to miraculously bring back one of our two family cars some sixty-four years later, there is no question I would choose our old Joey instead of the upstart Morris. How it would turn heads with the top down as it chugged towards one of Southern California's beaches! What a wonderful dream...

Mr Hemmings ... California, USA, September 2002

MEMORIES OF A 1928 LONG TOURER

I saw your request in the *Telegraph* on the subject of Jowetts, and I can tell you that I had one for a year between 1934 and 1935, but I do not know of its fate, but you might be interested in the following:

Mine was a 1928 Long Tourer, which I paid the princely sum of £9 for; it was slow but utterly reliable and easy to start with a sharp pull on the starting handle. I only had one involuntary stop just as I was entering Kidderminster; the car just stopped dead very suddenly, with the rear of the car rising off the road momentarily. Two large policemen appeared and tried to push me forwards into the kerb, but it wouldn't budge until they pushed it backwards. Looking underneath, I could see that the prop-shaft had dropped down and was jamming into the road surface. I lifted the front floorboards and saw that the bolts joining the two halves of the Hardy-Spicer universal joint were missing. Three 5/16-inch coach bolts were bought from a nearby ironmonger, which just took me a few minutes to fit and then I was on my way again.

I remember that the windscreen wiper was driven by a flexible shaft (like a speedometer cable) from a small pulley under the floorboards, connected by a small belt to a pulley on the prop-shaft. So wiper speed was controlled by road speed, and an adequate wipe could only be obtained by driving too fast for safety.

The car had no off-side front door, as it was a right-hand gate gear change and hand brake. The throttle pedal lay between the brake and clutch pedals. I taught my wife to drive in the Jowett, but one week before her test I changed the car for a Riley Nine, with central gear change and throttle on the right. In spite of all of this, she still passed.

G. C. Tysoe ... Pershore, Worcs, February 1996

1934 JOWETT SALOON REGISTERED AYE955

As a student in 1956 I bought a 1934 Jowett 7 six-light, four-door saloon. I bought it in the Saltley area of Birmingham for about £10; its registration number was AYE955.

It was in a fairly bad way and needed lots of welding to its wings. It had also been modified and it had lost its original petrol tank. This was replaced with a tank under the bonnet which fed to an AMAL carburettor originally from a BSA motorcycle (250cc!). The accelerator was a lovely concoction made from Meccano parts!

I ran it as a student at Nottingham University and also took it with me to the University College of North Staffordshire (now Keele University) in 1958 and ran it for at least another year. I regret that I cannot remember anything about its disposal, probably in 1959 when I replaced it with an Austin Cambridge of

1936 vintage. It may have been a case of terminal falling apart in several areas simultaneously, although I cannot remember scrapping it.

I can still clearly remember the 'winding up the flywheel' technique of driving, the 'winding up the steering joint springs' technique of steering and the 'look a long way down the road' technique of braking akin to 'a bulrush in a jam jar' and the headlights as comparable with 'a couple of fire flies in another jam jar'. It was my first car, nevertheless, and it served me well.

Dr Peter J. Harris ... Reading, February 1996

OUR FIRST CAR ... 'THERE WAS SOMETHING SPECIAL ABOUT OUR FIRST SET OF WHEELS'

This letter was published in a ladies' magazine called Chat in 1999, which I am reproducing here in full:

Our very first car was a 1934 Jowett 7 hp, a two-cylinder black saloon. We were newly married in the summer of 1948; and we bought it from a friend for £30. He sold it to us, he said, at a great sacrifice to himself. Later we were to query this on many occasions, but never have we felt such pride in any future car as we did in this one, our first.

All dressed up and ready to go, Joe, my husband, would depart to fetch the car from the barn of the friendly farmer where it was garaged. Later, much later, he would return dishevelled, bad tempered and oiled up, to greet an equally bad-tempered wife waiting for him. 'It wouldn't start,' he'd announce wearily.

Necessity had to be the mother of invention, and in this case, we devised our own starting plan, a two-person operation. Joe would lift the bonnet and, with the starting handle in place, be ready to swing. With my head under the bonnet, I would deftly hold together the two metal ends, looking like two rabbit ears, which closed the air intake to the choke. A quick swing and, a bit of luck, the engine would begin to chug away.

The barn held its own problems for us and the car. An anxious husband came home one night convinced that the propeller shaft had broken. After a sleepless night he returned next morning to find that the bumper was wrapped around a post holding up the roof. One day, opening the car door, two startled hens were confronted by an equally startled husband and, after much investigation as to the reason for scratching noises, a mouse was discovered very much at home in the depths of the front passenger seat.

We became experts at noise diagnosis, especially the ominous sound of a cracked cylinder head. These were made of aluminium and it meant a trip to London to have them welded. We were proud of our home-made heater, a copper pipe connected to the radiator. But our most essential piece of equipment on all journeys was the tow-rope, a rope that grew forever shorter as we trundled home behind faithful friends. A new rope was bought when three feet between cars seemed a little too close for comfort.

Why we loved this car so much beats us even today. It let us down when an excited new dad was on his way to bring his newly born twin daughters from the nursing home. 'We should have known this would happen,' exploded the new grandma. An hour later and it came chugging round the corner with a flushed and embarrassed dad at the wheel. But we were young and life was an adventure and the car was at the centre of it all. A three hundred mile camping trip to Cornwall was one of the many lovely times we had.

The fastest speed we ever reached was fifty-six miles an hour downhill – some going in 1950!

Sadly the day came when we had to part with the car, and preparations were made for selling. It was decided a new coat of paint – the paint to be supplied by a well-meaning friend. What he hadn't realised was that the paint, of unknown origin, was altogether incompatible with the original paint on the car, and a week later when it was presented to a prospective buyer, the paint was still wet! Not only that, but unfortunately, it had picked up a grey layer of grit on the way.

Advertised in a popular car magazine, our 1934 Jowett 7 aroused keen interest and sold for £60, the only car we've ever made a profit on. It was delivered to the buyer in North London: Joe came home sadly on the bus.

Mrs Isobel Hughes ... Southwell, Notts, April 1999

After Isobel's letter was published in the 'Chat' magazine, I wrote to the editor to see if they would put me in touch with her. This they duly did, and I received this charming letter from her, which I am sure also deserves to be published.

I was very surprised, but very thrilled to receive your letter this morning. I am pleased to enclose a copy of my article 'Our First Car' and a photograph, although I do apologise for the quality: it was taken fifty years ago. [*The picture was a very grainy side view ... NS*] But I do know it was registered AUA68.

Thank you for the copy of your magazine, it will bring back many memories for me. Sadly my husband died a few years ago, but we had many a laugh about the escapades we had in that car.

After the War it was the most wonderful thing to own a car. My husband had been in the RAF and was a POW for two years and he often told me how one of his dreams during his time in captivity was to be home again and driving a car in the English countryside. The Jowett to him was a dream come true.

BRADFORD-REGISTERED 1938 JOWETT 8 – DAK556

I was most interested to read the article in the October issue of the *Dalesman* concerning the Jowett Car Company, as the first car that I owned was a Jowett. It was a 1938 8-hp saloon which was blue with black mudguards; it had a registration number of DAK556. The first owner of the car was a Miss Jessie Hollingsworth of Farsley. I understand that she died early on in the Second World War, so the car was passed on to her brother-in-law. This man had never driven a car, so it was garaged during the hostilities.

Sid Drury bought his 1936 Jowett van after he came out of the army in 1946; he said he was fed up of marching by then! He paid £100 for it, and the log book told him that he was the thirteenth owner of the vehicle. Sadly, only part of the registration number is visible, as his leg obscures the numbers, but the letters are CWU.

Having served six years through the war I was demobbed in 1945 holding a licence to drive ALL classes of vehicle, though the only test I passed was for a motorcycle in June 1936, and the only thing I had to do to pass this was to ride round Leeds Town Hall for the examiner!

It was not until about 1954 that I was in a position to buy a car of my own, and I was offered the Jowett for £100. Considering the car would have cost about £250 when new in 1938, it seemed rather a lot, but it was a very low mileage car and my father assisted me in purchasing it, so I went ahead.

I remember that the car still had the old semaphore-type indicators, and only very small rear lights, as I fitted larger ones. I got a considerable amount of use from the car, as I drove it to the business I worked at in Wakefield daily (about 14 miles), also at the weekends for pleasure.

I remember on one occasion going out along with the family (wife and two children) and getting as far as Ilkley when a leaf spring broke, so I went into a school nearby and the caretaker gave me a piece of wood which I jammed in between the body and the spring, and went slowly home. I then went down to a 'car dump' and was lucky enough to find a spring to fit (most likely from a Bradford van) and replaced the broken one.

On another occasion I was coming home from Wakefield and the nearside cylinder blew off, but I was lucky as I was close to a Jowett garage near Morley and they replaced it for me. We had to be careful as we often took out my parents in the car, which made six occupants, which is quite impressive for only an 8-hp car.

I regularly took it over to Manchester and Liverpool which of course was before the M62 motorway was built over the Pennines. Also on one occasion we went to Northampton to see some relations and then down to London, so you can see it got a fair amount of use.

I ran the car until 1956, when I traded it in for a Hillman Minx, when I got £40 trade-in for it – I wish I still had it now.

I hope you find this interesting, but please do excuse my handwriting; I am ninety-three years old and past my best! [*I can assure you his handwriting is better than mine! … NS*]

I have a photo of the car somewhere and would lend it to you if you wish. [*Yes, I asked for it! … NS*]

Frank Procter … Pudsey, West Yorkshire, November 2009

Frank wrote to me again in early December with two pictures of the car, one from the rear, the other from the side together with this note:

I am enclosing two photographs of my 'travels with DAK'. One was taken in the Yorkshire Dales, the other in the Sherwood Forrest on our Nottingham and London trip. My children on the photographs are now grandparents themselves and my wife and I are now great-grandparents (4).

MEMORIES OF A 1936 JOWETT VAN REGISTERED CWU*** AND JAVELIN REGISTERED PRF35* ALL THE WAY FROM AUSTRALIA

When I came out of the army in 1946 I'd had enough marching. I decided to buy a car. My father's friend who owned a garage said, 'You need a van to be able to get red petrol.' I paid £100 for a 1936 Jowett van; the log book showed that it had had thirteen previous owners.

My best friend Dennis' (ex-RAF) father had a milk distributing business and always used Jowett vans because they were always reliable in the frost and snow, and never let him down. So Dennis and I always did the maintenance on our cars on a Thursday night before going for a pint.

I remember that I'd planned an Easter holiday to the Lake District in 1948. On the Thursday I discovered a leak in the manifold coming from the carburettor to the engine mounting where someone had used an over-sized spanner and worn the aluminium pipe paper thin. I took it to an aluminium welder but he was too busy to do it and suggested that I bought a six-penny tube of aluminium solder from Woolworths. It did the job and was still in position when I sold the Jowett in November 1949, as I was migrating to Australia.

I went to the Car Sales Yards to see what prices were like and saw two Rolls-Royce cars for sale, the first was a 1934 example which sold for £99, and the second was a 1939 car which went for £800. This was because there was still rationing on white petrol and larger cars became less attractive. I managed to sell the van for £95, so only lost £5 after three-and-a-half years of motoring with it, together with a total of £3 15 shillings being spent on it! On arrival in Canberra, Australia, I met a friend who was the agent for Jowett cars out there; he had also been a racing driver in South Africa before that.

In 1997 I visited a Machine Show in a town called Temora, New South Wales, 150 miles from us in Canberra. There was a large display of working tractors with examples from Russia, Germany, Italy, France and Great Britain, mainly from the pre-war era. Tucked away amongst them I saw a Jowett flat-twin stationary engine operating a lathe.

I remember that when I took the Jowett van to be sold in Leeds before setting off to come here, I had a long look at the two Rolls-Royce cars that were for sale and promised myself that one day I would own one myself. So I set this as my goal and I'm pleased to be able to tell you that I have owned a Rolls-Royce Silver Shadow for the last seventeen years. I still have to say, however, that I enjoyed my ownership of the Jowett van more than any other vehicle I have owned.

Please could you send me a copy of your book *Jowett 1901-1954*? I enclose my cheque to cover the cost. Good luck to you and your club.

Sid Drury ... Canberra, Australia, September 2002

I sent a book to Sid, and he sent me this reply together with a Christmas card:

I received your book OK and I think it was great!

Please find enclosed a picture of my mate Dennis' wife stood beside their Jowett Javelin which must have been taken in about 1953 or 1954. My old mate also had

Sid's best friend was called Dennis. He owned a Javelin. This is a picture of Dennis' wife stood next to it. Once again, the number plate is partially obscured, but you can see a little more with just the last number missing: PRF35*. The back of the picture is interesting, as this young lady clearly was a little obsessed with her weight, etc. The note reads, 'I am not as big as I look, it must be the way Dennis has taken it. I am now 8 stone 12 lb and used to be 7 stone 4 lb, size 36-26-37'!

This 1938 Jowett 8 hp, which was registered DAK556, was the first car that Frank Procter bought in 1954 for £100; this seemed expensive at the time, but he said it was a very low-mileage car. He worked in Wakefield at the time and used it for work each day and for weekend use. He ran the car until 1956, when he traded it in against a Hillman Minx.

a couple of pre-war Jowett vans, and as mentioned previously, we used to work on them together every Thursday evening when we were both in Leeds. Sadly Dennis passed on six years ago.

Jowett Cars Ltd should never have closed down – they took their eyes off the ball and look what happened next!

Sid Drury … September 2002

There was a small picture of Sid standing next to his 1936 Jowett van, but Sid's leg blocks part of the registration number, the letters of which are CWU …

The other picture shows Dennis' wife standing at the front of their Javelin, once again she partially obscures the number plate, but you can see a little more, with just the last number missing: PRF35*. The back of the picture is interesting, as this young lady clearly was a little obsessed with her weight, etc. The note reads, 'I am not as big as I look, it must be the way Dennis has taken it. I am now 8 stone 12 lb and used to be 7 stone 4 lb, size 36-26-37'!

HOME-MADE JOWETT SHOOTING BRAKE REGISTERED KY8578 (BUILT ON A *C.* 1934 VAN CHASSIS)

When I was visiting my family in Yorkshire at Christmas, I came across your article in the *Dalesman* magazine about Jowett cars.

My father, Cyril Foster, had a Jowett van and in about 1948 he converted it into a 'shooting brake' in the back garden of his parents' house in York.

I enclose a photo of the original van, then during the conversion (my father in the vehicle) and then the finished 'brake' with his brother, Christopher Foster, together with a couple of photographs of our family (my mother, Ivy, my sister Malane and myself) camping with the car in Whitby. My parents slept in the tent, but Malane and I slept in 'Jowina', the pet name we had for her. She was always classed as one of the family!

Sadly, her renovated body was extensively damaged by a Leeds Corporation Tram in, I think, 1950. I don't know if Dad repaired her sometime after or not, but I do know we then had a Norton motorcycle and sidecar. I am a bit hazy about the dates as I was only three in 1948, and at that age things are just taken for granted.

I do hope these photographs are of interest to you. [*You bet they are! … NS*]

Sue E. Foster … Gatehouse of Fleet, Castle Douglas, January 2010

NB. I had the pleasure of meeting Sue in July 2010, as she was camping again in Whitby. She told me that she was five at the time of the crash and that she had been thrown out onto the road by the impact of being hit by the tram. Sixty years on and she still remembers the screeching of the tram's metal wheels so close to her.

The Foster family camping in Whitby in about 1950.

Cyril Foster proudly standing with the completed Jowett shooting brake.

MEMORIES OF BRADFORD OWNERS

THE SLEEPING BEAUTY BRADFORD

With reference to your article in the *Daily Telegraph* about Jowett cars, you may be interested in my old Bradford Jowett which was registered RMY622, which I owned or knew about between 1959 and 1964.

I was on Colonial Service stationed in Mombasa, Kenya, with four children in UK boarding schools; we needed inexpensive transport when we came home on leave. When we came on leave in 1959 we stopped at Wandsworth Common, London, with my father for a few days before coming down to our house here. I looked for a cheap second-hand car in the local Wandsworth Borough News and saw the Bradford advertised for £150. It was located at Wardley Street off Garratt Lane, Wandsworth, my father strongly advised me against going there as the street had a reputation even before the war as a place where policemen always went in pairs! No doubt it has been much regenerated since then, and nothing untoward happened to me when I went to buy the car.

It had been well cared for and had been fitted with an immersion heater in the cooling system for plugging into the mains at night and a chromium-plated tetrachloride Pyrene fire extinguisher, which I still have. The engine of course was the Jowett two-cylinder horizontally opposed type and the body was an estate kind with windows in the sides which my wife made curtains for, for camping use. It had a chassis to which wooden cross-members were bolted with a stout wooden floor.

That summer we set off for a camping holiday in it to Cornwall, four children, tents, bedding, kitchen etc., all very weighty as we were used to camping African Safari style. In 1959 there were no by-passes on the A38 and the road through Launceston involved a very steep hill, so my eldest son, John, was at the ready to jump out of the back doors and push, or as a last resort put a brick behind the back wheel. However we made it up and duly set up camp at Trevose Head. Next morning going to the village there was a terrible noise from the engine and I dreaded that I might be stuck with the family in a broken-down car miles from home and with a very slim purse. Not very hopefully I lifted the bonnet and saw with amazement that one of the two plug leads had come off and we were running on one cylinder!

Between leaves I came to an arrangement with Castle Garage, Tangier, Taunton, to store the car and have it ready each time we came back. In 1960 I lent it to my brother-in-law, who was also coming home on leave from Mombasa with his family. He arranged for the AA to drive it up to meet his ship at Tilbury Docks. The young lady from the AA who did this driving said it was the most unusual car she had ferried, but she had enjoyed the drive.

The car did us great service and was a favourite with our children and their friends. When fetching the boys from their prep school at Sparkford there were cries of 'here comes the fish van' from their school mates as we came through the park of Hazlegrove House. There was even a theory that it had no engine but was propelled by the passenger's feet through holes in the floor! These were the days when there was great snobbery about parents' cars, and when we were asked to take a nephew to a rather posh prep school in Gloucestershire, a friend said, 'You cannot possibly take the boy in that car – he will never live it down!' In fact the Bradford settled in very well with the Jags and Bentleys. On 'leave Sundays' there was quite a competition to travel in it!

In 1963 I sold it to another family in Mombasa and they continued to use it as 'a leave car' when home in Tiverton. When it was parked in Tiverton it was run into by a lorry and I heard that the repairs to the hand-finished doors had cost the insurance company dearly. In turn it was sold to a colonel in Taunton who was a Jowett fan. Some years later, when coming down the A303 from Sparkford, we saw the Bradford parked behind a garage near Tintinhull.

We still often use this road so we recently stopped and asked if they knew anything about it. The garage is now much bigger and is still owned by the same family, and they said that they not only knew the car, but they still had it! They promised to get it out some time and photograph it for us.

The garage is Taylor's Coaches, Townsend Garage, Tintinhull, near Yeovil, Somerset.

Douglas Tyrrell ... Clayhidon, Cullompton, Devon, April 1996

On rereading this letter again in 2008, it made me wonder if this Bradford had still survived at the garage for another twelve years. I rang the number quoted above to find the garage is still run by the same family, but the coach side of the business had ceased. They rang me back to say that they had kept the Bradford for many years, but did in fact sell it 'some years ago', but sadly they did not have a record of to whom.

A BRADFORD – FAR FROM IDLE!

My late uncle Sydney B. Clarkson worked for Jowett for a number of years after the First World War. Latterly he was a director of Bradford Garages which, as I remember it, was an associate company of Jowett Motors and was virtually their Sales Division. Whether my uncle was ever a director of Jowett itself I am not sure, but think possibly not.

In April 1948 I bought a new Bradford van (navy blue plus side windows but no rear seats and registered FAK746) from my uncle at Bradford Garages, and I collected it from Bradford and drove it south to Hampshire myself. This was the first car I owned, and although hideously uncomfortable, I loved it dearly and had an enormous amount of fun with it. Like all Jowetts it climbed fantastically, and was super-economical on fuel, which was a great attraction in those post-war years of rationing. I kept it for nearly four years, and in February 1952 I sold it to Barnett & Small in Farnham, Surrey (who are still in existence), who were the local Jowett dealers, it had then completed nearly 30,000 miles. I changed cars (being on the point of getting married) and wanted something more comfortable. My uncle promised to get me a Javelin, but by the time it had come through, I had already bought myself an Austin. My uncle was rather disappointed, and I had great regrets because, though I liked my rare and unusual Jensen-bodied A40 sports car, the Javelin was a very excellent car and would eventually have been more suitable with the advent of family.

Sadly my uncle died in August 1952. I did, however, buy a second-hand grey Bradford basic van, registered NPD35, from Barnett & Small of Farnham in 1953 in order to drive to and from work. Sadly it was a failure, and surprisingly, I had much mechanical trouble. I sold it again after only six months in Hackney, East London. However FAK746, my original Bradford, had been a huge success with negligible trouble, except for one rather frightening moment on a winter's night on a steepish hill, when the brake linkage came apart, but somehow the gearbox eventually brought us to a stop safely. We repaired it ourselves by the roadside!

On my recommendation a friend of mine, Dick J. Dunford, bought a new silver Bradford van with sliding side windows, registered KXO487, in early 1949 from Barnett & Small of Farnham in Surrey. This was an even better specimen than my own and had a superior trim and other refinements. For the next four summers until 1954 Dick Dunford and I plus our friends took one or another of our Bradfords on two-week long-distance reconnaissance camping trips abroad. They were really most unsuitable vehicles for the job in hand, particularly from a bodywork viewpoint, but in the event they performed admirably for their period and specification, and proved very reliable but were uncomfortable. We always had a crew of four, drawn from a group of us comprising nine men and two girls (all still alive in 1996 as far as I know!) and all of whom drove in shifts. These included Dick Dunford's two younger brothers and one of his sisters.

Both Dick and his great army friend, Norman Shaw, were tank soldier veterans of Alamein and the Italian Campaign. I myself had been a tank man in the Normandy landings, so we were used to 'primitive bivouacking'. The camping conditions were of necessity pretty Spartan, and as the Bradford roofs would not take roof racks, all our equipment, luggage, cooking kit etc., had to travel inside with us, which made things very cramped.

One great compensation of those days back in the late forties and early fifties, was that camping sites were scarce except on the Riviera coast and major tourist areas, and regulations were lax. This enabled us to camp more or less where we wanted, even by the roadside in rural areas, which suited us just fine. This of course would not be possible today.

Our first trip in July 1949 in my Bradford FAK746, was to France, Switzerland, and the Italian Lakes, then the Riviera coastline and back to Paris, and we covered 1,946 miles in the two weeks on a successful and largely trouble-free trip. The all-in cost to each of the four of us was an incredible £32 inclusive, and we did not exactly stint ourselves on food and drink – which just goes to show what you could do in 1949! I note that the ferry charges across the Channel were not included in this figure, but from memory I believe they were approximately £25. In 1950 we were all short of money so we had to make do with a week's camping in Cornwall. We took my vehicle again, FAK746, but the weather was atrocious and we resolved to go abroad in the next year.

This we duly did and in 1951 we made two trips – one in each vehicle and different crews. On the first trip in May 1951, Dick Dunford took his silver Bradford KXO487 and I accompanied him with one of his brothers and Norman Shaw. The object was to retrace some of the Dunford/Shaw steps taken during the Italian Campaign. We crossed to Dieppe, and after visiting friends in Port Audemer (Normandy) went on to Zurich, St Moritz through the Alps St Gothard to Venice, Bologna, Florence, Forli, Rimini, Ancona, Assisi (the furthest point south), Pisa, Turin and back through the Bernina Pass, then back to Paris, including an exhausting drive of over 450 miles in a day! Then back through Calais after 2,500+ miles in two weeks. This was a marvellous journey, but very tiring in such a basic vehicle as the Jowett and on bad roads of that period of time.

In July (of that same year) we were off again from Newhaven – Dieppe, but this time it was in my vehicle FAK746 (for the last time) and with a different crew – and without Dick Dunford for the first time. This time it was the French Riviera coast, where I joined the trip by flying out to Nice. We went along the French side of the Pyrenees to the Basque country around St Jean de Luz and Biarritz, then back through Bordeaux, Poitiers, Angouleme, Tours, Chartres, to Paris and back via Calais, a distance of approximately 1,900 miles in fourteen days, as we usually did. This was a lovely trip and much more relaxed in beautiful weather, and completely trouble-free. I sold FAK746 in 1952, so never went again.

However, Dick Dunford and Norman Shaw, with different crews, went back to Italy with the silver Bradford on two or three occasions between 1952 and 1954 with great success and enjoyment. I think that on one of the trips they got as far as Rome. Looking back to those far off days, it was all great fun and the sturdy little Bradford vans provided us with such enjoyment. Dick Dunford was the moving spirit behind our trips and he was an excellent driver and mechanic, as also were his two brothers. He was also a good linguist, which helped greatly, and a good photographer. [As published by me in the May 1998 issue of the Jowetteer ... NS]

A GAY OLD BRADFORD!

My husband and I moved to Yorkshire two years ago, and I recently came across an old copy of Yorkshire Life which had your article on Jowett Cars in it.

In 1953 my husband was doing his National Service, just after we had married at the age of twenty-one; he had been deferred as he was serving his apprenticeship. He was travelling most weekends from his station in Lincolnshire to our home near Burton-on-Trent on a BSA motorcycle, which he found very cold in the winter.

In early 1954 he went back to camp after a weekend at home on his BSA and returned the following weekend in a green and black Jowett Bradford van, the number plate being GAY7; he had bought it from a garage in a village called West Bridgeford near Nottingham.

We had some very happy times with GAY; my mother acquired a double cinema seat for the back and my husband ran copper pipes from the radiator into the back for warmth for the rear passengers.

We sold GAY in late 1958 or early 1959, trading it in for a Hillman Husky at our local garage in Church Gresley near Burton-on-Trent.

Mrs Betty L Watson ... Weldrake, York, 1997

BRADFORD VAN REGISTERED LLG125

I have been a Jowett owner since 1963 when, as apprentice marine engineers in Liverpool, a friend and I bought a Bradford van to be repaired and used as transport on the local 'works outings' which we made from our College to such places as Cammell Laird's and English Electric. We had access to workshop facilities both at the College and in the shipping company's hostel where we lived, so we felt well prepared. Just as well.

Our enquiries led us, via a 1938 Daimler saloon with a seized-up Wilson pre-selector gearbox, 'If you can move it you can have it', we couldn't, to a Bradford registered LLG125, lying in the corner of a coal merchant's yard in the Aigburth area. It had been taken in payment of a bad debt by a local coal merchant; it had flat tyres and a 'hangdog' expression, but apparently was complete. The strongest point in its favour was that it could be ours for £5, but even so, as we were earning £1 2s 6d per week, this was still a sizable investment. The money changed hands, and we examined our prize a little more carefully. We was robbed!

As we opened the rear doors, the remaining stock of apples, cabbages etc., which had been left by the previous owner, disappeared as the now rotten wooden floor collapsed. However, the chassis frames which we could now see clearly appeared to be in fairly good order apart from some corrosion due to the apples. The rod-operated brake mechanism and exhaust were not. The lower parts of the steel rear quarter panels were suffering from tinworm, the engine was solid, and the battery was naturally past its best. We applied wind in the tyres and towed it home.

As marine engineers with more enthusiasm and energy than caution, we removed the remaining body easily (only about six bolts and it was quite light as I recall), and set about restoring the chassis. This was chipped, welded, wire brushed and given a coat of red-lead and really looked quite smart. With this rapid start made the rest slowed quite a bit.

The engine was stripped with the aid of lots of paraffin, and was not in too bad condition apart from one burnt-out exhaust valve. A new spare was located in an ex-Jowett agency in Birkenhead and fitted. The gearbox seemed OK when we examined it by removing the 'lid', so we left it alone. Our failure to notice that the studs securing the cover to the box also located the selector rod guides, led to an interesting journey across Liverpool one wet night, without the benefit of the clutch or second gear. At college, we machined the king pins back to parallel and made, fitted and reamed a set of bushes to suit them as they were now non-standard.

Meantime back at the hostel, we examined the body, which without a floor lacked a certain amount of structural rigidity. Some framing was replaced and the cloth top was given a coat of weatherproof paint, but there was little more we could do until the body was back on the chassis and fitted with the floor. The electrical wiring was lacking continuity, where it existed.

The mechanical brakes offered a challenge. All the clevis joints were very badly worn and one oil seal in the back axle had failed, allowing the brake assembly to be soaked in oil. This had preserved the mechanism but destroyed the effectiveness of the brake linings. We solved this by boiling the brake shoes in washing powder solution which claimed to 'remove oily stains'. A full set of clevis forks and pins were manufactured in our workshops, fitted, greased and adjusted. The oil seal (a sort of coil of cork strip) was replaced and everything seemed OK.

The re-assembled engine was refitted in the chassis and the radiator filled. It leaked. We removed it and took it to the hostel workshop and spent many happy hours filling it with water, marking the leaks, draining it, soldering them up and repeating the process. I recall there was a lot of exposed solder eventually. A new silencer was fabricated at college and fitted to the remains of the exhaust pipe.

With the aid of about eight colleagues at the hostel, the body without the floor was refitted. The rusted rear quarters were patched with plates cut from an old filing cabinet; we saved up and bought a tin of 'battleship grey' household paint which really improved matters and people asked when it would be finished.

With the floor still missing, it would be fairly easy to do a complete rewire – if only we had some wire. The college had an electrical department from where we scrounged lots of bits of red 'mains' wiring; this was quite effective but a little confusing as it was not possible to colour code. Still, Bradford wiring is simple – isn't it? This caused problems one dark night on the M1, when the voltage regulator – didn't.

With the rewire complete, we could start to think about starting her up again, but the battery was not only flat (it had a little liquid in some of the cells, which may have been acid – but who knows?), but it rattled. We removed the plate clusters by melting the 'tar' compound on top, washed the plates and cleared the 'bits' between them, swept out the dust, re-assembled it, filled it with acid, charged it and hoped. It worked – sort of.

Since the battery was suspect (at best), we needed a starting handle; once again the college resources were plundered and we came up with a 1-inch diameter bar of black mild steel which we forged into the required crank, machined up and welded on a driving 'dog' to fit the engine. It weighed quite a lot! It was not until much later that we found out that the original article was much lighter, being made out of about 5/8-inch diameter material with sleeves to fit the hole in the bumper. But that was after I had broken a bone in my hand when it backfired on me.

As the engine had not run in living memory, we turned it with the plugs out for ages until we felt that the oil pump had done its best to deliver the goods to the parts which should be reached, and the petrol pump had moved the contents of the tank to the float chamber. Plugs in, ignition on, one brisk turn on the handle and it all worked. Boring really, and it was a shame that there was still no floor! The din from the engine attracted the builders on the site next to the hostel. We explained about the lack of floor and they gave us an 8 x 4 sheet of 5/8-inch ply that they had been using to mix concrete on – it fitted perfectly. We sawed off the overhang beyond the rear doors and made bench seats along each side in the back. At this time there were no panels at the ends of the benches, but we used the spaces underneath to keep our tools and the 'left over' bits.

With everything working, the next hurdle was insurance and the MOT; insurance was only money (we didn't have much), but the MOT was interesting. This was before the days of 'rolling roads' for brake testing. The original seat runners had rusted away, so we had made and fitted to the seats some little metal plates with pegs on them, which plugged into steel strips with a row of holes to allow adjustment, fitted to the floor.

The mechanic checked everything else then drove round the back of the garage to test the brakes. We heard the squeal as the brakes did their stuff (they really worked quite well), but the van did not reappear. We walked round and found the mechanic pinned to the steering wheel by the seat. This had tipped forward on its pegs and been securely wedged in position by tools etc. which had slid forward from their hiding places under the benches.

He seemed to take this personally, because he then jacked up the front of the van to about four feet off the ground and put a prop under the front axle before removing the jack. He spent a lot of time admiring the beautiful shiny phosphor bronze king pin bushes and the colourful wiring loom and poking the pretty redlead finish on the chassis, but eventually he grunted and issued the Certificate.

Taxed at last, we had about six months use before we resumed our careers at sea. We made trips to Newcastle, Manchester and to my home in Sussex as well as general use in the Merseyside area. We eventually sold the van for £12 10s 0d to a local pop group. We never heard of the van or pop group again.

Ian Howell ... Eastbourne, East Sussex, May 1996

JOWETT 7 AND BRADFORD MEMORIES

I was interested to read your letter in the *Saga* magazine, because at one time I owned a Jowett 7-hp saloon for about two years. I sold this privately to an acquaintance and then I purchased a Bradford van from a garage in Settle. I used to use this for business for about two years. I fitted side windows and put a bench seat in the back, as by then it was old enough to convert into a passenger vehicle without having to pay purchase tax on it.

I maintained both vehicles myself with an assortment of friends; we did everything including several de-cokes, which was a Saturday morning job. I also remember fitting Wellworthy piston rings to the saloon, which, as you know, was made with a wood frame and fabric-covered body, mounted on a chassis built like a tank. The Bradford still had a wooden frame and aluminium body and still with a heavy chassis. I remember going up Sutton Bank in the Bradford with five of us in, and it stopped halfway up, with a great deal of panic from the rear passengers, who rapidly got out as the Bradford was still rolling back with the handbrake full on. I was left on my own with the foot brake hard on also. The AA man, or was it the RAC, came down, there was usually one on duty at the top of the bank, and told us that most probably the petrol boiled in the carburettor, so he suggested that I waited another five minutes for it to cool down and try again. My passengers had walked to the top and after a short while I started her up again and drove to the top with no more problems, I then collected up my passengers and we carried on our way again.

Baines Brothers in Harrogate were the Jowett agents and stocked a very good range of spares, I went to school with Colin Baines, the son of one of the brothers, and he eventually took over the business. I think he still has a house in Harrogate, and no doubt he would be a mine of information for you. [*I could not trace him at the time ... NS*]

I also remember one stroke of luck I had, we were going to Morecambe for a day out with two friends, we were in the Bradford and a half-shaft broke just as we were approaching Long Preston. I went to the local garage, and talk about luck, they had one in stock! They did not, however, have anybody available who could fit it for me. So I had the problem of withdrawing the broken half from inside the axle casing; but with a kiddies fishing net cane with the end split open and held with matches, I managed to push this in and withdraw the broken shaft. I then fitted the new one and we were on our way again in less than an hour.

Another point that I am sure you will find of interest is that I worked for Tommy Wise during the time that he and Tommy Wisdom were driving together and winning their class in the 1950 Le Mans 24-hour race in a Jupiter. Tommy also took part in the Monte Carlo Rally in both a Javelin and a Jupiter. Mr Wise owned the St Peter's Garage and the Spatax taxi firm in Harrogate in partnership with John Harris. Tommy was a great character, really very impetuous; he used to come into the office and out again like a hurricane, always with a cigarette in his mouth, which I think got him in the end for he died quite young.

I remember one trip I did with him driving, we were going to York from Harrogate in the Jupiter, and we had twenty minutes to catch a train in York which was twenty miles from Harrogate. We actually made it to York in time to buy a ticket and board the train; that had to be the ride of my life!

Harry B. Bancroft ... Harrogate, August 2000

BRADFORD MEMORIES FROM CANADA

I was interested to see your letter published in the December 1999 issue of the *Dalesman* magazine, regarding Jowett cars – I bet you did not expect to get a reply from Canada!

However, I owned a Bradford shooting-brake in the early 1950s. The body was wood-framed, but had an unusual slatted roof which could support the weight of an adult and was the delight of my young children. The body sides were also unusual as they were in timber also, with a door on the side just behind the driver's door to gain access to the rear of the vehicle, doors at the rear also opened.

I am sorry that the photo does not show the front-end of the car; this is a laser print of the only picture I have of the car. You will see that it is standing outside Porch House in Sleights, where the family lived for a time. I can also tell you that the car's registration number was PV7874.

I am the son of A. H. Walker, who started one of the very first automobile garages in Yorkshire back in 1901; my mother was also one of the first lady drivers in Yorkshire. The garage was located at Crescent Avenue, Whitby. The garage was knocked down many years ago and the site is now occupied by the Post Office sorting office. I spent most of my life working at the garage, apart from the war years, working at and later managing the garage before retiring to Canada.

I can't remember the Jowett ever giving much trouble except when it developed a bad steering wobble at certain speeds – this was before anybody had tumbled to balancing wheels to cure this. The result was the snapping of the steering column just as my daughter drove in from Whitby and pulled up at Porch House with no steering. She later said that it had been shimmying all the way home from Whitby.

The only other Jowett I can remember in the area was a sort of two-seater that was owned by my friend H. Mortimer Batten, the wildlife photographer and author, who lived for a while in Goathland, long before its glory days.

I am a bit of an antique myself, being ninety-two this year, and I still have my 1925 driving licence, when I bought my first car, an Austin Seven with a Gordon-England two-seater body. It was a speedy little car, and would actually do 50 mph! I now drive a Volkswagen GT1 (which is a souped-up rabbit) which is quite lively and pleasant to drive.

Arnold Walker ... Salmon Arm, British Columbia, Canada, January 2000

Sleights, near Whitby, is where I live; I checked with the Post Office and found that Porch House still exists. I took my Javelin down and parked it outside as close as I could to the original picture with his Bradford. I took a picture of my car and sent it to Arnold, which he was delighted with.

ONE OF MY REQUESTS FOUND ITS WAY TO TENERIFE!

While on holiday in Tenerife last month I was most interested to read your request in an English magazine, which had been left behind in our hotel, asking for information on Jowett cars.

Whether you include the Bradford van or not I am not sure, but that was what I had. In 1957 I had a motorcycle and sidecar combination but saw a late example of a Bradford for sale at £200, which I bought. I found that the nearside cylinder had some damage and the battery was weak, but I soon sorted things out.

Then came the conversions to it, first I cut two large apertures in the two side panels and the rear doors and fitted new windows, then painted it blue and red, which were my regimental colours. I then fitted carpets in the back and an old bus seat. I cut the back off the passenger seat and fitted dowels to the bottom and slots at the back of the seat squab, so it could be easily lifted out so that it gave easy access to the rear of the van. I then made the seats easily detachable from the floor, so while on holidays we could remove them and lay the mattress down to sleep on; the mattress was stored on the back, rolled up when we were travelling.

Next came a Trico tandem wiper kit and screen washer (water pistols!), the two headlamps were made double dip with focusing attachments, two saucer-sized rear lamps with 24-watt brake bulbs. These were handy at night if anybody tried to tailgate me; a few quick taps on the brake pedal soon saw them drop back! I fitted a length of copper piping along the edge of the dash and connected it to the cooling system which acted as a heater until I bought a re-circulating one.

When the exhaust went, I fitted twin straight-through exhausts, they came out of the lower rear body panel, with chrome-plated ends to the copper piping, and this gave it a great noise from behind.

By this time our camping equipment was taking up a lot of room, so I made an all-steel trailer, so it could be all loaded up into that, giving the rear passengers much more room.

My next mod is one that you will not want to read about, but I will tell you anyway. I wanted to fit an Austin A30 or A35 engine and gearbox, but I could not get hold of a good unit so I got a Morris 8 one instead. The accommodation of this unit was quite straightforward and the performance was greatly improved. I clocked 70 mph on a level straight, which was unknown in a Bradford, but on the hills pulling the trailer it dropped right back.

Later I had a dealer contact me, as he had heard about the Bradford; I traded it in to him against a Bedford Dormobile. After this came a Humber Hawk and fourteen-foot six-inch caravan, but in 1972, on doctor's orders, I was told to take things easy, which I am still trying to do.

Gordon Simms ... Wetherby, West Yorkshire, March 1996

A BRADFORD POLICE VAN REGISTERED FFW201 – NEEDED FOR HIGH SPEED CHASES!?

In the early 1950s I had a fruit and vegetable business in Lincoln which was close to the Headquarters of the Lincolnshire County Police. At that time they had a fleet of Jowett Bradford vans which they used as Black Marias. In 1954 or 1955 these were taken out of service and they were disposed of by tender, so this was how I came to purchase FFW201, for the sum of £240, or thereabouts. They were used to transport six policemen, two in the front and four in the rear in steel bucket seats facing inwards so they tended to have a 'rear end droop'. But I am pleased to say that mine was, I was told, only used to carry police uniforms and court files.

When I first got it, it was painted in police dark blue so I had it hand painted a two-tone colour scheme with cream on top and the bottom was coffee brown and it looked really super.

She served me well for about three years and gave me very little trouble and had a kick like a mule when it came to climbing hills; it only needed a de-coke once and nothing else. It was a 'B' of a gearbox until you got used to it. I have to say I loved her both for business and pleasure and she would bomb along all day at 45- 50 mph with no problems and she never wanted a drink – just fresh air.

If you publish any of what I have written in your club magazine, please could I have a copy also. Do you have any records in your club about what happened to FFW201, as I would love to know what happened to her? I did see her once in a car park in Woodall Spa a couple of years after I had sold her, but I could not find the owner to talk to.

I only parted with her because I needed a bigger van for the business and a growing family and also because my wife never got used to changing gear in it.

Ron Parker ... North Hykeham, Lincoln, January 2001

BRADFORD VAN REGISTERED JWR52

I read the article in the October issue of the *Dalesman* magazine about Jowett cars with great interest.

My father farmed at Delves Ridge Farm, Darley, which was a mixed farm with dairy cattle and sheep, which ran to about 400 acres.

During the war years we ran an Austin 12-hp van, but after the hard winter of 1948, where chains had to be used regularly on the wheels, it was worn out. There were no Land Rovers in those days and the farm van had to do everything. The van was replaced by a Morris car registered CMU824 and a trailer. This was not a success, as it could not do the work that the van did. So in 1949 we bought a new Bradford van registered JWR52, which had a two-cylinder engine, which when running, it had a very distinctive pop-pop-pop sound! It had a large carrying capacity but the suspension was rather suspect, particularly when it was fully loaded, or more often than not, overloaded with 10- and 12-gallon churns of milk in the back, or full of sheep! I think we paid about £550 for it; it was always outside, and never garaged.

In 1952 the farm was requisitioned by the Ministry of Defence to enable them to build the HMS *Forest Moor* Wireless Station. The outcome was that we had a farm sale to sell off all the farm machinery etc. The beloved Bradford was sold for £252 to Mr J. R. Houseman of Hollins Farm, High Bristwith, Harrogate. He ran it for almost 20 years between 1952 and 1970, he said it was also utterly reliable for him, and he never had a spanner on it! [*I wish I could find a Jowett like that ... NS*]

Barrie Liddle ... Harrogate, November 2009

BRADFORD UTILITY REGISTERED NNB540

I was interested to read your piece in issue number 78 of *Down Your Way* magazine regarding Jowett cars. You may be interested in our experience in running a Jowett Bradford Utility deluxe. I bought it from a second-hand car dealer in Leeds in 1959 for £125; I then sold it in the spring of the following year.

This vehicle was ideal for our purpose, we were newly married and living in Horsforth, Leeds, and it was used very much for holidays on a budget. We had the idea of having all our belongings into two metal trunks, which, of course, easily fitted in the rear of the vehicle. We then set off on our grand tour of the Scottish

John Allan relaxing in the shade in front of his Bradford Utility deluxe registered NNB540 whilst on a camping holiday in Scotland, this picture being taken at the Loch of the Lowes. This was John's second Jowett, which he paid £125 for in the late 1950s; he ran it for just over a year. His first Jowett as a pre-war saloon registered DNW573, which was laid-up during the war. His daughter said that John was a real Jowett enthusiast. Both these Jowetts were purchased second-hand in Leeds, where John and his family lived for many years. (Allan)

John Allan having a wash and brush-up on his Scottish camping holiday, the rear seats had been removed and curtains put up across the side windows, as he and his wife regularly slept in it, but they also used bed & breakfast accommodation. They also toured the Lake District sleeping on mattresses in the back; they said the accommodation was very basic, but great fun! (Allan)

mountains, sleeping either in the back with the rear seats removed and curtains on the windows or on some occasions in B&Bs. I remember we also had similar weekends in the Yorkshire Dales and Moors, Northumberland and the Lake District. I remember we were nearly washed away in a storm at the top of the Wrynose Pass one time while we were in the Lakes. The Jowett also took me to work on occasions and to my parents' house on the Wirral on a regular basis.

It was so reliable and the only expense it put us to was to replace a broken petrol pipe whilst in Fife, which was probably due to the rough terrain we were crossing at the time. As you will realise, our Jowett was fully utilised for a full summer and gave us much pleasure. We had no qualms about parting with it when we did for £25, as the new MOT 'Ten-Year Test' was just being introduced later in the year and it was unlikely that it would have passed on its steering and brakes, also the headlights were dim even when it was new!

The two pictures, enclosed, are for you to keep, the first shows the Utility in the Highlands and the other which shows the Jowett from the rear was taken in your area, at the top of Blue Bank, Sleights, Whitby. [*Yes, it is a mile from my house ... NS*]

I am now over eighty years old so I do not think I should join the Club, as my driving days are over since I had a stroke, so my wife drives our Micra! I think that the specification on my Bradford was better than on some of the other models, as it had twin wiper blades, a step/running board and a chrome radiator shell. [*Yes, the Utility Deluxe was the top-of-the-range model ... NS*]

Mrs O'Grady's uncle owned a Jowett Bradford van while she lived in Australia between 1956 and 1959. He loved it and had very little trouble with it even though the climate in North Queensland is very hard on any car. The enclosed photo shows her with the Bradford and her uncle on Christmas Day 1957 outside his home at Townsville, North Queensland.

I can also add that my father-in-law had three pre-war Jowetts in succession, as he was suspicious of anything made outside Yorkshire! We have evidence of that, as we have on our kitchen shelf a clock he removed from the dashboard of one of his Jowetts and it still gives us perfect service! I regret that we do not have any pictures of these three Jowetts, but we have a note that states that the second car was registered DNW573. He was a great admirer of these cars and delighted in leaving other cars standing on the steep narrow lanes of the Dales. This second car was laid-up during the war and he was greatly impressed by how easily it started up again after its long rest.

John Allan … Sheffield, June 2004

BRADFORD CAPERS IN OZ

My uncle owned a Jowett Bradford van, while we lived in Australia between 1956 and 1959. He loved it and had very little trouble with it even though the climate in North Queensland is very hard on any car. It is either pouring down with rain in the wet season, or very hot and dusty in the summer, many of the roads being unmade at that time.

My husband and I borrowed it once to go to a drive-in movie, but that's the only time it has been used for that purpose!

Reading your article in the *Dalesman* brought back many happy memories for me. The enclosed photo shows me with the Bradford and my uncle on Christmas Day 1957 outside his home at Townsville, North Queensland.

Mrs Cynthia O'Grady … Guisborough, October 2009

MEMORIES OF
JAVELIN OWNERS

A JAVELIN FONDLY REMEMBERED BY ITS OWNER, NOW LIVING IN THE USA

I have just finished reading your book *Jowett 1901-1954*, and as a past Jowett owner I thought I would tell you about my experience with my Javelin in the early 1960s.

In the summer of 1963 I traded in my 1945 Austin Eight at a used car dealer in Southsea, Portsmouth, for a 1952 Jowett Javelin.

The registration number that sticks in my mind was HJU688, though the only photo I have found of it looks more like 683. I know that isn't a Portsmouth registration, I was thinking maybe it was Leicester registered, but I may be mixing it up with my first car. [*Mike, in fact, is quite right, HJU688 was chassis number 20229; the registration is a Leicestershire one that ran from January-February 1952 ... NS*]

At the time I bought the car, Jowett parts and handbooks were still available from Howden Clough, and I remember getting parts and information from there. The main troubles I had initially were misfiring in the wet, always a chronic problem on Javelins, I think. In later life, the gearshift linkage at the column broke – I had that welded. Then later on, a more serious problem occurred in the transmission, which would then only let me engage, I think it was 1st top and reverse gears. I had to drive the car to South London, where they overhauled the transmission for me. I also had them rebuild the engine at the same time because it was burning oil. I don't remember what the repair bill came to, but I know I had to plead for money from my father! This was in the winter of 1963/64, I think, but it may have been a year later.

Shortly after that I went to work for Vauxhall Motors in Luton. Gerry Palmer was an executive there at the time, but I had minimal contact with him, and at the time I didn't know that he'd designed the Javelin.

The 1½ litre J

IT'S NEW RI

ett JAVELIN

T. THROUGH

On the August Bank Holiday weekend in 1965, the Javelin was written-off in a major collision on Buster Hill, just south of Petersfield on the A3. It's not there now; a faster dual carriageway road has replaced it. We were almost stationary at the time, slowly climbing the hill in traffic behind a slow truck, when we were hit by a speeding Morris 1100 coming the opposite way.

As it happens, my parents were away on vacation, and were due home the next day, so we'd used the space behind the armrest in the front seat of the Javelin to stow a glass bottle of milk and some eggs. This all added to the glorious mess inside the car after we had been hit. My passenger broke his jaw on the dash, but though badly bruised I was not kept in hospital.

The car was written off and was towed to a car dealer in Petersfield. I went out to see it a few days later and was shocked to see how badly damaged it was. It literally broke its back when it was towed away. I still have photos I took at the time and feel we were lucky to survive the crash, and I am grateful that the car was as strong as it was.

So now you know what happened …to my Javelin, and I have always worn seat belts religiously since that day. (The Javelin didn't have any of course – I'd always thought I'd see the collision coming and be able to avoid it.)

Mike Tedrake, Rochester, Michigan, USA … July 2000

TWO JAVELINS - ONE NUMBER PLATE!

Following your letter in the Motoring agony column of *The Daily Telegraph* on Jowett cars, I can give you some information on two Javelin models.

The first was a 1953 PE black standard model which I bought in 1963 just before the parts department closed down in Batley; they operated this service for ten years after the closure of the factory. This car was registered HBO250 and lasted until around 1965 when it suffered terminal unfixable body rot around the rear torsion bar mountings which tore out of the body, these were visible by removing the rear seat squab.

The second Javelin I bought for six pounds ten shillings without engine or gearbox from a garage in Marple, Cheshire, that dealt in Jowetts. The engine and gearbox were taken out of HBO250 and fitted into the 'new car'. This then lived on the same number plate until August 1966 when it failed its MOT and was scrapped into a scrap yard at Heaton Mersey, Stockport.

So both cars were scrapped within two years. The only mementoes I have are the white plastic cover with the Jowett emblem on which was the radio blanking plate and the Jowett-issued maintenance manual.

R. A. Wilkinson … Newbury, Berks, February 1996

A BIT OF BOTHER WITH JAVELIN EPR308

I write in response to your letter in *The Telegraph* dated 17 February. I had the above Jowett Javelin from about May 1963 to April 1965. I am not sure when it was built, but I think it was either 1951 or 1952. I purchased it second hand from a garage in Christchurch, Hants, for £110. I covered a fairly high mileage as during this period I was undergoing flying training in the RAF and at various times was living in Hants, Dorset, Wilts and Suffolk. It became increasingly difficult to keep going and it finally broke down when I was on holiday on the Isle of Wight, a few days before I was going overseas for two years. In the middle of Ryde an engine mounting broke and the whole transmission system locked up, blocking the traffic in the main street. I went to the pub and got a group of people to help bounce the car to the side of the road. No mean feat with a Javelin!

I left the car with one of them who said he was involved with a scrap yard on the understanding that he would dispose of it. Unfortunately I didn't tell the Vehicle Licensing Authority! In 1967 I was contacted by the Ryde police asking for details of the person I had passed the car on to. It appeared that the 1965 tax disc had been used on a car which had been involved in some illegal undertaking. I described the pub as well as I could, and a vague description of the main characters involved, all of which seemed to confirm information that the police already had. It seems that old Jowetts never die, they keep coming back to haunt one!

John Child ... Chichester, West Sussex, February 1996

THE HALF-CROWN JAVELIN

Further to our telephone conversation and your article in *The Somerset County Gazette* at the weekend, I enclose my one and only photograph of the Javelin my boyfriend won in a raffle in 1965. [*This was a very grainy side-view, which would not reproduce here ... NS*]

We went to a very rough and ready barbecue on the Quantock Hills in September 1965. In the corner of the field was a very sad heap of car being manhandled by the various people at the party. They were not treating it with much kindness and were all rather rude about it. However, Robin Shawyer and I bought a raffle ticket for 2s 6d and went off to another party in the area. There seemed to be endless parties in those days! The next morning our cook's husband, who had been doing the electrics at the party took enormous pleasure in telling me we had won the car.

This was extremely exciting, but also posed a bit of a problem. I was only fifteen so could not drive, and Robin had only just passed his test. However, some kind person towed the car back to my home, where we scratched our heads as to how we could make it go! We cannot quite remember who did fix it but somebody got it going, and presumably it was properly taxed and insured by Robin. One of our memorable jaunts I recall was when we went off to a party at nearby Cothelstone and on the way home we managed to take a wrong turning in the dark. We ended up going down an extremely narrow flooded lane. By the time we reached home we both had very wet feet as the water had come into the car in waves around our feet.

I must have gone back to boarding school sometime in mid-September and Robin must have driven it around during his gap year. He thinks he sold it in January 1966 for £35 before going off to do VSO in Botswana. I wonder what happened to the car, it was registered MUW ???

Mrs Carolyn Moore (née Mitford-Slade) ... Taunton, September 1998

A SALES PERSON'S JAVELIN REMINISCENCES

I have just been reading, with much pleasure, your book *My Car was a Jowett*, given to me by one of my sons for my recent seventy-seventh birthday. I also have *Jowett 1901-1954* as a gift from a previous birthday. I didn't own it but I did drive a Javelin for a couple of years and will leave it to you to decide whether any of the following is of interest to you. [*Of course it is, Mr Angell ... NS*]

Around 1951 I joined a small, privately owned, engineering company in Slough called Ronald Trist & Co. Ltd. The owner and 'hands-on' Managing Director was a Mr T. L. Wakley, a fine engineer and a great leader of men. He was looked on with respect, indeed affection, by all who worked with him. The company's business was in the industrial steam boiler world where it had developed a range of water-level control equipment. These had been modernised to fit in with the transition from manual coal-firing and steam pumps to automatic stokers, oil-firing and electric-feed pumps, then taking place. To install and subsequently maintain this equipment on a regular contract basis, the Company employed some fifty Service Engineers covering the whole of the United Kingdom and Southern Ireland. These were one-man units, each with a van carrying tools and spares.

In the fleet of Service vans there was a good number of ex-WD vehicles, half-tonners with just a canvas sheet at the back, but the rest were mainly Bradford vans. I think Mr Wakley may have had an interest in Clarkes of Pirbright, the Jowett agents who supplied the Bradford vans, as all the new ones came from there. He himself drove a Bentley, but soon after the Company switched to Austin vans.

In 1955 I achieved my immediate ambition and was appointed Technical Sales Representative, responsible for the Company's business in the counties of Oxfordshire, Buckinghamshire, Berkshire, Surrey and Hampshire. As such, I needed a motorcar and I didn't have one. Not long after our marriage in 1949 we bought a 1935 Ford 10 Tourer but eventually sold it when it became increasingly unreliable and major bills loomed. We then bought a MSS Velocette motorcycle (500cc) and when our first son was born, added a Triumph Tiger 90 with Watsonian child/adult sidecar to the fleet! As an ARP despatch rider at sixteen, I had ridden both solo and sidecar machines during the war years.

Normally, a Technical Sales Representative would provide his own car, the Company making him a loan if necessary which would be paid back out of his subsequent allowances and expenses. For some reason I was offered the use of a Jowett Javelin, formerly driven by the Assistant Managing Director, Mr D. S. Prince. The car's registration number was TPJ395, and was a sandy bronze colour known as Golden Sand, with red leather upholstery, a bench seat and a column gear change. The heater was a wire-wound element like a one-bar electric fire with a fan behind it to blow heated air into the car.

Was this a Javelin standard item or not, I wonder? The car's suspension was fabulous, far in advance of most other cars of that time. More than once I looked into the rear mirror to see an aspiring overtaker floundering all over the road on exiting the previous corner.

With the advent of the Suez Crisis, petrol rationing returned and there were various dodges to try and stretch every gallon as far as possible.

Over-inflating the tyres was common, as was coasting in neutral with the engine switched off. No steering locks or brake servo systems to worry about in those days. Returning along the A30 from a day's work, I could usually slip over the top of the hill at the Jolly Gardener pub in Camberley with 50 mph on the clock, into neutral, engine off and coast all the way through Bagshot, past the Hero of Inkerman and the Fighting Cocks pubs and as far as The Cricketers before I had to restart the engine and engage gear – by which time the road speed was down to about 10 mph, but there was far less traffic on the roads in those days.

The Javelin only let me down once, and threatened to do so on one other occasion, both times were whilst we were on holiday in 1956. Because of petrol rationing we had arranged a weeks' holiday in Swanage, just a few miles from Bournemouth where I could work on the Friday and then travel to Swanage with minimal use of the precious fuel. In the event it was all unnecessary because rationing ceased a couple of weeks before we were due to go.

However, whilst on holiday, I had to attend a business meeting in Central London – W1 actually – and left Swanage in the Javelin early one morning to get there. After quite a few miles and on the A30 – yet again – I noticed that the engine water temperature gauge was going down, reading colder. I knew that a couple of miles further on there was a small garage with a workshop so I pulled in there, only to find a hand-written notice on the door stating, 'The Management regrets any inconvenience caused, but it has gone to have its hair cut!' Opening the bonnet, I soon found that the cause of my trouble was that the bottom hose had pulled off the stub connection of the radiator. So it was out with my own tools and the hose was soon back in place and the Jubilee clip tightened firmly. But then I needed water; it so happened that I had a lemonade bottle in the car with perhaps a pint of water in it. As I recall the Javelin had a large radiator and needed something like 9 pints to fill it. I looked for a tap with no luck, but did find a urinal with a drilled pipe running along it to flush the wall periodically. This was controlled by a tap in the supply line, from which the handle had been removed – presumably to prevent unauthorised use! An adjustable spanner soon took care of that and I filled my lemonade bottle umpteen times from one of these tiny holes, going to and fro from the car to transfer the water to the radiator. I got quite wet in the process from all the other holes! Eventually the radiator was full, I turned off the water and drove off with the proprietor blissfully unaware of all that had been going on while he was having his hair cut.

Arriving at my meeting in London (quite a stuffy affair) and late, I was eyed curiously by the Chairman, who commented that I looked as though I had been dragged through a hedge backwards. I told him about it afterwards.

With petrol rationing finished we decided to extend our holiday by going to Wales and call at friends who lived in Caerphilly. The approach to Caerphilly was up a desperately steep and long hill with a crawler lane for heavy trucks on the ascent. It was an awful day, pouring with rain, cold, damp and spray flying everywhere. Halfway up I lost one plug with water, and still with a long way to go developed a misfire. Had it cut out completely I do not think that it would have made it. The following day our friends tried to get the local garage to come out but they declined when they heard that it was a Javelin. So we dried things off ourselves, got the car started and let it run for a while until it was warmed up, and normal service restored. I had no more trouble thereafter.

In 1957 my own, and first new, car came through after many months of waiting. It was a Series 111 Morris Oxford with a dished bonnet; the body is still sold today in India where it is called the Ambassador. I covered 97,000 miles in four years in that car and it never missed a beat. At that time of course there was not a single motorway in the country. But it had numerous grease nipples which required attention every 1,000 miles. Years after trading it in, it could be seen on the A4 running between Windsor and Heathrow where the new owner worked.

I do not know what happened to TPJ395 as I handed it back to my employers when I got my Morris Oxford, but I never saw it again after that. I remember that the design was ahead of its time in many respects, particularly the suspension. It needed further development to iron out its weaknesses, but sadly for Jowett this never happened.

Despite the road traffic conditions that prevail today, I still enjoy my motoring and cover about 14,000 miles annually. I have a Rover 420 Turbo diesel which is a joy to drive and economical with it. Why the model is so down rated by the alleged experts I do not understand.

Incidentally, I was in Aden with Cable & Wireless in 1947-48 but did not ever see a Javelin there, so presumably they came in after my time.

Thank you for the two most interesting books, I wish you well and all who continue to drive Jowetts.

Stanley G. Angell ... Andover, Hants, November 2003

MY JAVELIN COST ME MY NEW JOB!

I was most interested in your letter in the *Saga* magazine, as it brought back so many happy memories of a faraway world! I bought my Jowett Javelin in 1956, it was second-hand, but only just – it had done a very low mileage, and was in excellent condition. I was delighted with it – lovely appearance, nippy engine, walnut fascia, and everything that one expected with a 'classy' motorcar. The only trouble initially was that my wife hated the gear-change system. However, she became used to this, and it wasn't till I had the car that I discovered the real problem! It was a wonderful 'runner' as long as the weather was fine, but if the weather was very wet, it was a different matter!

The flat-four engine put the spark plugs far too accessible to the spray from the road, and one by one the plugs would short, and the cylinders gave up! The first occasion this happened was when we were going to Ireland to spend a holiday with my parents. It had been raining all the way up to Liverpool. We got halfway through the Mersey Tunnel, and then, to my horror, the engine began to falter! We just managed to crawl out on one or two cylinders. The next time was a year later; I was due to attend an interview at Ealing Hospital for an important post. I had to go to a funeral down in Salisbury during the day, and my interview was not until the evening. It had been raining all day and we were within two miles of the hospital when she said she had had enough!

I left her on the side of the road and managed to get a lift to the hospital in a lorry, and when I arrived at the hospital I was very bedraggled and very late. Needless to say I didn't get the job, but managed to get another lift back to the car. She took me to within two miles from home and then died! I then had to walk the remaining distance, arriving home in the early hours of the morning.

All went well for the next year or so, and then we had planned another holiday in Ireland. My wife didn't want to go, so I planned to drive her down to Salisbury where she was to stay with a friend, with my little daughter, while I took the boys over to Ireland with the car the following day. We had just left Salisbury on our way home, when the universal joint on the main shaft gave up. The car was towed all the way home, where we left it with my local garage. We went to Ireland the next day – by train!

When I returned the poor Jowett was taken in part exchange for a second-hand Hillman Husky – a poor exchange I fear!

Dr Robin Burkitt ... Farnham Common, Bucks, August 2000

THE JAVELIN WITH TANK SPARK PLUGS

My wife has shown me your letter in the *Saga* magazine; 'This will bring back some memories', she said. Indeed it does, so I'll reminisce, but forgive me if I slip up in the detail.

I passed my driving test in Blackpool in 1946 (yes, British School of Motoring, courtesy of the RAF). So when I wanted to part exchange my motorbike for a car in 1955 I'd had ample time to study the market, and went looking for a Jowett Javelin.

The local Jowett agents in the 1950s were Buntings of Harrow (near the Granada Cinema), with quite a small showroom just big enough for two new cars inside. Outside they had two or three used models squeezed between the window and the pavement. Two petrol pumps with overhead pipes to stretch over the cars and footpath to fill up your car on the road, not allowed nowadays. The area was an affluent part of North West London; nothing came cheap, but customer service from this small garage in advice and labour was first class.

I found the Javelin I wanted at Alperton, a few miles away; it was a 1948 model registered EX6328; and the asking price £395 which I thought was over the top. However, it had a factory reconditioned engine numbered R1163; this was important to me as I knew Jowett had made two mistakes when the car was new:

This 1948 Javelin registered EX6328 was bought by Mr Rimell in 1955 from the by then ex-Jowett agents Buntings of Harrow (near the Granada Cinema) for £395. They had a small showroom just big enough for two cars; outside they had two or three used cars squeezed between the window and pavement. Two petrol pumps were in front of the showroom with long overhead pipes that stretched over the cars and pavement to fill cars up on the roadside. Needless to say, Health & Safety regulations put paid to this practice many years ago – it's amazing we have all managed to survive these dangerous times! (Rimell)

1. It had hydraulic tappets, not itself a fault, but nobody outside the factory could set the system properly. Buntings said that if a microscopic particle got into the fluid, it failed. I heard another explanation elsewhere that it was difficult to ensure no air bubble got into the system. Left alone this self-adjust tappet system would likely be no trouble. But it was not to be because of fault.

2. The white metal big-end bearings did not allow sufficient oil buffering and were failing after a few thousand miles. New owners hardly got over the big-end trouble when they were faced with tappet problems. The official remedy was to scrap the hydraulic tappet system and replace with the conventional manual-adjust.

So I was pleased to see that EX6328 had had this done, and equally the salesman seemed keen on my Ariel bike with its springing at both ends and its 500cc engine – so I inflated my expected part-exchange allowance, and we made a deal.

Once it was mine I found that EX6328 had been a company car in Manchester, so I wrote with a SAE to the secretary, and by reply learnt that it had been fitted with a new engine. They had passed it on to their London depot two weeks before I'd bought it and were surprised to hear that it had been sold on. I found out why – it guzzled oil – but luckily I found out the cause: a loose mechanical fuel pump flange. When I tightened it up the oil consumption dropped to zero.

I wanted to start work on the car and needed a hub puller to remove the rear wheel hubs; this is when I found out that one was not supplied with the tool tray in the boot. Buntings had a puller in stock but they needed it in their workshop, but had six made to special order, selling the excess to customers at 'about cost price'. I think I paid almost ten pounds for it and was told that the large diameter fine thread had to be case-hardened, hence the high price.

At my first major breakdown I was touring in Wales, delightful for holidays when dry, but even drizzle in Wales makes little brooklets flow over the roads and the whoosh as I hit the two inches of water lifted the rubber seals from the front of the spark plugs; both sides of the engine were dead. A local garage towed me to the village; overnight they dried out under the bonnet, fitted new leads and let my pal and I sleep in armchairs after filling us with sandwiches and cocoa. The bill next morning was less than what we had expected and we were grateful for our Welsh hospitality. Then on, but the continued rain meant worry.

After the holiday I sought help from Buntings ... 'Yes we have the only real answer,' they said, 'Tank plugs'. They laid out four on the counter in front of me. 'How much?' was my next question. 'Six pounds each, £24 the set, but they are double that in town (London).' A normal plug was five bob, or four to a pound. You could also buy platinum plugs to special order at fifteen shillings each, but Buntings pointed out that the fifteen bob plugs only had tiny inserts of the precious metal, whereas each of the ones in front of me had three solid platinum bars each at about 1 x 1 x 10 mm. The next rainfall might be much more pricy than the Welsh experience, so I bought them. At the time ordinary sparking plugs were etched away by the spark a lot more than in modern times, and the gaps had to be set at each service. Not so with platinum plugs, which didn't erode. Also the tank spark plugs had the same reach and screw pitch as the factory plugs, they were taller and had a metal body all the way to their hollow tops in which fitted the HT leads sealed in metal tubes. I didn't doubt when told they would run underwater, but I never put it to the test!

One other mod I did at this time comes to mind; I like an engine to start first contact on the starter. The two carbs and the engine layout in the Javelin could cause the engine to make extra turns to prime the carbs before it would start. I plumbed an electric pump in parallel with the mechanical fuel pump, wiring it to the same supply as the ignition light on the dash. This worked very well. Switch on ignition ... click, or click-click, no more. After a few seconds it would start first time. Then the ignition light goes out, and until switch off it runs on the mechanical pump.

I also remember that in the first year or so I fitted a set of Michelin X radials, including the spare. They were new on the market at the time, claiming high mileage, more mpg and super grip. The latter was verified when I found myself in a line of traffic struggling to climb a frozen Alconbury hill. A van in front slipped back on each forward attempt, the next time he'd come into me. I put EX6328 into third, slipped the clutch and sailed away non-stop to the top on those Javelin 16-inch X-radial fitted wheels.

After about four years of comfortable and on the whole trouble-free motoring with EX6328, a local garage owner asked if he could sell me a car. 'Only if it's a Javelin better than the one I have,' I said. 'Come and see,' was his reply. There it was, beautiful! DEB465 was a 1953 deluxe Javelin, one of the last few made, now six years old but little used. I was told I could keep whatever bits I wanted from EX6328, so I kept the engine and the wheels with their Xs. I hadn't gone out of my way to get this later model, but when I realised all the advances in design I knew I should have gone after a later model much earlier. EX6328 had hydraulic braking only on the front wheels, cable pull on the rear. On DEB465 it was all four hydraulic, (plus mechanical hand brake on the rear of course). Not only that but the newer model had twin leading shoes on the drums, bringing vastly better braking efficiency. Also the grease nipples on the 1948 model suspension had been replaced by compressed rubbers on the newer model – quieter and no servicing needed. The dashboard was walnut (the old one was metal) and a factory-fitted radio. Some of this may be attributed to the deluxe version. [*Yes, the deluxe had the walnut dash; the Standard still had a metal one … NS*]

I said my first major breakdown was in Wales, and I was about to have my second. I went to stay with an old friend in Swaledale and parked DEB465 on a steep slope at the side of the house. The handbrake was tightly on, cable operated, and to make sure the car didn't move I parked in gear. (I don't remember if it was forward or reverse). The next day the gearbox didn't work, wouldn't engage. With help I got the car jacked high on piled limestone and took the side panel off the gearbox. A gear selector fork was bent; I got it out, hammered it straight the best I could and put it back … and it worked.

I enjoyed four years of motoring with DEB465 and the gearbox gave no further trouble, but I didn't park again in gear. I played hockey and regularly transported fellow team members in winter, so I did not keep the car pristine inside. A snow slide from a house top dented the roof. After eight years with memorable Javelins I bought a Herald Estate in 1963 (no more hockey).

Typing this has refreshed pleasant memories, so if it's of interest to your club members so be it.

C. W. Rimell … Spalding, Lincolnshire, October 2000

JAVELIN CHICKEN COOP IN RHODESIA?

We went to live in Southern Rhodesia in 1957 and bought a second-hand Jowett Javelin saloon car. I seem to remember that the previous owner was a doctor. It was a very comfortable car with leather seats and a useful shelf on the back of the front seat. We did, however, often have problems getting it started, and on several occasions had to arrange a lift home after an evening out.

The local garages had no expertise with these cars, but fortunately we discovered a motor mechanic called Les Tempest, who at some time had worked at the Jowett factory in Bradford prior to him emigrating over here, and he was able to keep the car serviced and running for us.

We sold the car in 1959 so it is probably housing chickens in someone's backyard now!

Mrs B. M. Evans … Leeds, February 1996

1. This is the oldest Jowett in existence, being a 1913 example; there were forty-eight cars built by the Jowett brothers from 1910 to 1916. At that time, car manufacture ceased, as the factory switched to the First World War effort. Three of the first forty-eight cars were on display at the Centenary Rally, the others being another 1913 example and one from 1916.

2. This is the 1916 Jowett, the third-oldest Jowett in existence. It is owned by Mike Koch-Osborne, who is the grandson of William Jowett, one of the Jowett brothers who founded the company. The picture was taken at the seventy-fifth anniversary of the Yorkshire Gliding Club Rally in July 2009.

3. When Jowett production recommenced after the First World War, it was at a new purpose-built factory at Five Lane Ends, Idle, which at the time was on the outskirts of Bradford. The first model produced was the Short-Two, which had a dicky-seat at the back. This 1927 example now lives in Devon. This picture was taken at the Jowett Car Club Rally in Bideford in May 2009.

4. The next Jowett model to be introduced alongside the Short-Two was the Long-Four; this had a proper hood together with Perspex side-screens that could be fitted in wet and cold weather. This picture was taken at the Jowett Car Club Rally in Bideford in May 2009.

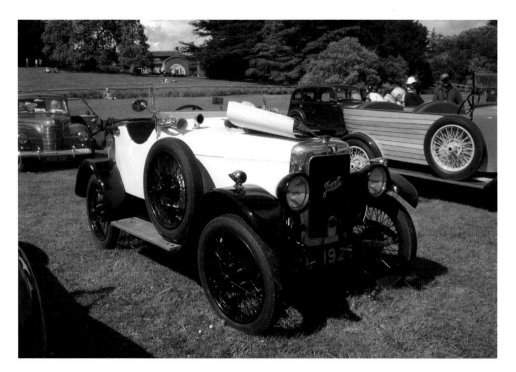

5. From the very early 1920s, the Jowett brothers, and others, entered Jowett cars in reliability trials and hill climbs, etc. One such person was Major Johnstone who took part in many events as early as the Scottish Six-Day Trial in June 1922. This is his 1923 sports model, which is now owned by William Jowett's grandson, Mike Koch-Osborne.

6. Open a Jowett bonnet and see what happens! This car is a 1935 Curlew model, which, of course, is fitted with the standard 7-hp flat-twin engine.

7. This is a 1935 example of the model known as the Weasel. It was a sportier model with twin carburettors. Sadly, there are only a handful of survivors.

8. This very attractive tourer was known as the Eagle-Special Tourer, being built on a standard 1934 chassis. (Fearn)

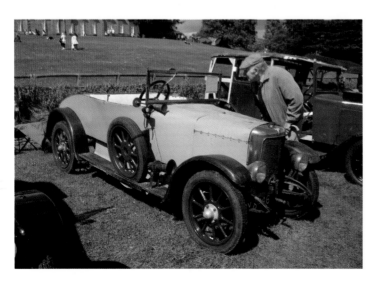

9. A 1929 Long-Four minus its hood and side screens, the note on the windscreen giving details of the car has caught the attention of this enthusiast.

10. This 1934 Long Saloon known as 'Belinda' has been owned by the same club member since 1956, who paid the princely sum of £25 for it. The car was used to tour Italy in 1967 before being laid-up during the 1970s. The car has had a complete rebuild, returning the car to her former glory.

11. The Jason of 1935 was Jowett's answer to the fashionable streamlining craze of the 1930s with its racked radiator grille. Needless to say, the average northern Jowett owner threw up their hands in horror at such a futuristic vehicle, and it was quickly withdrawn and replaced with the stop-gap models, the Plover and Peregrine, until the more conservative Jowett 8 and 10 were introduced in 1936. The Jason and the later 10 hp both used the new flat-four engine while the 8 continued using the long-established flat-twin. In total, 105 Jasons were built (the deluxe model), and thirty Jupiters were built (the standard model). Two Jasons still exist and both were at the Centenary Rally!

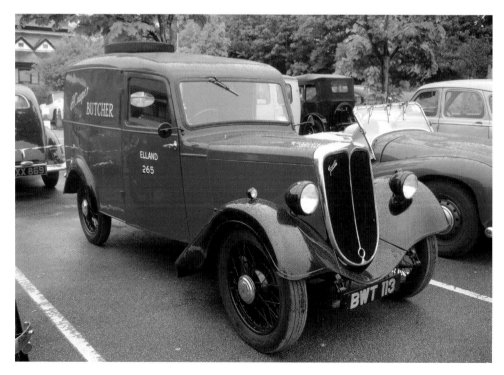

12. A 1936 7-hp van. Pre-war Jowett commercials are ultra rare, as clearly most were used as workhorses with no thought of restoration in mind. Note the spare wheel on the roof to allow more storage space within.

13. An ultra-rare colour picture from the 1951 Monte Carlo Rally, which shows Robert Ellison getting out of the class-winning Jupiter to receive his trophy. As can be seen, this was a formal affair, so there were no boiler suits and berets being worn here! His team mate was Bill Robinson, who was also a garage proprietor, his being Mill Brow Garage, Dalton, Cumbria. (Ellison)

14. This surely has to be the best way to transport a trio of Bradfords! Everybody in the hotel car park who had a camera (me included) ran over to take this picture. It is carrying the full set of Bradfords: a van, Utility and lorry.

15. A beautifully restored 1951 Bradford Utility on display. This vehicle went on to win the concours award for the best Bradford at the rally.

16. A nice pair of Bradfords: a 1952 van and a 1951 lorry.

17. A 1951 Javelin all the way from Denmark. Note the non-standard sun visors on the front of the car.

18. A Javelin in 'Heartbeat Country' in September 2009. This car is in fact the last Javelin sold in the UK, registered in early 1954. (Heseltine)

19. A trio of Javelins seen at the Jowett Car Club Rally, Bideford 2009.

20. A very nicely restored 1953 Jupiter.

21. The 1952 Jupiter in racing trim that was brought to the rally from Denmark. This is a very well-known Jupiter that had been raced and rallied extensively by its previous owner in the UK. It is now being raced again in Denmark.

22. Another overseas Jupiter attending the rally.

23. The 1951 Sommer-bodied Jupiter. This was the only special-bodied Jupiter that this concern built. It used the standard Jupiter front-end but then had a coupé body with sloping rear, reminiscent of the Javelin design. This is such an attractive car, and it was a real pleasure to see it for the first time!

★   ★   *"With spurs, would climb trees"*   ★   ★

"FOCUS"

THE LONG TWO-SEATER

WITH FOUR-WHEEL BRAKES AND TWO DOORS

The picture gives but a faint idea of the smartness of this car. The seats are wide and comfortable, and the rear compartment, when not carrying passengers, takes care of a large amount of luggage.

Side screens of glass and a smart hood make a coupé in bad weather. Chromium plated opening screen with safety glass and full de-luxe equipment.

Finish : Royal Blue with trimming to match.

For full specification see page 18.

Price, Coachbuilt only, £145 (ex works)

JOWETT CARS LIMITED · IDLE · BRADFORD · YORKS·

24. This is another special-bodied Jupiter: an Abbot-bodied car; this car was not at the Centenary Rally, as its owners came in a standard-bodied Jupiter that they also own. This picture was taken at the Jowett Car Club Rally in Bideford in May 2009, where it won the award for the best special-bodied Jupiter at the rally.

25. The R4 Jupiter parked in the Cedar Court Hotel car park, Wakefield with the present owner, Keith Patchett (left) talking to Phill Green. Phill worked for Jowett Cars Ltd in the Experimental Department and worked on that very car nearly sixty years ago! The R4 Jupiter was displayed at the 1953 Earls Court Motor Show, which was Jowett's last-ditch attempt to keep trading. This had a different less-complicated chassis than the existing Jupiter and the body was to be built in the then experimental fibreglass. Sadly, only three prototypes were built before the company ceased trading. The first one was built in steel followed by two examples in fibreglass, the steel car still exists, but this car is the remaining fibreglass car; the other example does not survive.

26. A view of the R4 Jupiter and the Mark 2 Jupiter parked on the rally field at Cannon Hall, Wakefield. They certainly attracted a lot of attention.

27. The 1952 Le Mans winning Jupiter always attracts a large crowd of interested enthusiasts as soon as it parks; this picture was taken by me at a brief lull in the numbers! After the race, the three team cars were dismantled and thrown onto the company scrapheap, the chassis being cut in two. A young enterprising employee bought enough parts from the heap to rebuild one again. Ironically, the Jowett engine was fitted later, as he could not afford one at the time!

28. This is the second special-bodied Jupiter built by Harold Radford pictured next to a standard-bodied Jupiter. The other Harold Radford car was supplied new to Gerald Lascelles, the Queen's cousin.

29. I have greatly admired many motoring personalities over the years, but I added a new one to my list in 2008 in the shape of Bill Ebzery of Australia. Bill and his team rebuilt three 1949 Bradford lorries from the remains of abandoned vehicles found in barns, etc., across Australia. The Bradfords were then sign written WAIT, AND, SEE in memory of the WAIT & SEE Jowetts that crossed Africa in 1926. Bill and his team then undertook a remarkable trip with them by crossing Australia west to east from Perth to Sydney, which was an incredible 5,500 km. Part of the route included crossing the vast Nullarbor Plain, a treeless barren desert hundreds of miles long. (Ebzery)

30. This is me in my Jupiter taken at the North Yorkshire Moors Vintage Vehicle Weekend in July 2008. We had just arrived at Grosmont station and had to wait for the level crossing. My wife, Jane, jumped out of the car and took this super picture of the *Sir Nigel Gresley* going past.

31. My 1952 Javelin, this car is most unusual as it has a proper sunshine roof fitted, only one of a handful that were done. The first owner of the car was a dentist in Blackpool who liked open-topped motoring. I was told by the person from whom I bought the car that the dentist had said to Jowett's that he would buy one provided that they had a sunshine roof fitted for him. I have not been able to confirm if that was correct or not, but it is certainly a very professional job, so I would like to think that it was correct.

32. The Centenary Rally in Wakefield attracted many overseas members; around sixty came from Australia and New Zealand, plus others from Northern Ireland, France, Sweden, Denmark, Canada and nine from the USA. This picture was taken on Monday 24 May, just prior to the rally near to my home in Whitby. It shows my 1953 Utility with me on the left with long-suffering wife Jane on the right with Dave Burrows from Pittsburgh who visited us before we set off for the rally. Dave and Judy have a fantastic Jupiter, which has won many awards in the USA. (Judy Burrows)

33. 'Drive it Day' in Whitby on 25 April 2010. the North East Section of the Jowett Car Club met for Sunday lunch and had three Jowetts on display: my 1952 Jupiter, a 1934 Saloon and a 1954 Javelin. The Javelin was the last one to be registered in the UK and has recently been restored to a very high standard.

ANOTHER JAVELIN WITH A BROKEN CRANKSHAFT!

I saw your letter in the *Daily Telegraph* and I thought I should let you know about my father's old Javelin. It was a black deluxe example with beige interior and registered MXH826. It was unusual in that it had been very professionally converted so that it had a large sunroof; although I was only a child at the time, I do remember that this had been very professionally done. It was used every day by my father to commute to the Bristol area to and from work.

My father was not the original owner of the car, but he will have bought the car in about 1953 and he kept it until 1957 or 1958 when he traded it in for a horrendous Vauxhall Victor in primrose yellow!

There is not a lot else I can tell you about the Javelin, but I will list what I can remember:

It went like stink (for the time) and my father used to talk about its low centre of gravity. It broke its crankshaft at one stage and the family was called together to talk about an economy drive, as this was NOT in the budget!

The liners round the cylinders started leaking and for a period it had the spooky habit when you turned it off of ingesting some water which promptly turned to steam. It would continue to run very gently as a steam engine after the ignition was turned off. I suppose it could have been a blown head gasket, but somehow I connect the problem to sunken liners.

As a family we used to spend quite a bit of time in Europe and I do remember it had a problem with cooling on mountain passes. I think probably it normally ran very cold, and for this reason the local garage suggested my father ran it without a fan. On long mountain passes, working hard at low speed, it had to be rested from time to time.

The only other memory I have was being with it in Spain; the Spanish had a major problem with it since there is no letter 'J' in Spanish. I think we will have been there in 1953 or 1954.

Writing this has made me realise that cars have come a long way since then!

Stephen Sampson ... Rotherwick, Hants, February 1996

JAVELIN NXN6

I read your article in the *Daily Telegraph* with interest, as the ex-owner of a Javelin registered NXN6. This was my first car which I purchased in 1961 at the age of twenty-one from a garage in Ashton-under-Lyne, which went out of business many years ago. I ran the Javelin for approximately a year, during which period it was reasonably reliable, but suffering from terminal rot. However, this was not the cause of its demise.

On a run back from Skegness to Manchester the usual waving between Jowett owners took place. Somewhat surprisingly this developed into waving from most cars going in the opposite direction. At this point I decided to stop and see what all the fuss was about. An inspection of the engine revealed that a core plug had come out with a corresponding loss of water. Repairs were attempted at the roadside, as was the want in those days. Nothing stemmed the flow of water until, eureka, it was found that the old half crown was slightly larger than the offending hole. This was the perfect remedy and with its high silver content was easily peened into place. The journey was resumed but the radiator had sprung a small leak during this mishap.

The following winter, two nights of sub-zero temperature, combined with a lack of anti-freeze due to the leak, led to disaster. On the first night I remembered to drain the cooling system. On the second night, returning home from club-land in the early hours I chanced it. The result, doom and gloom, the aluminium jacket round the pots was fractured. Due to the state of the bodywork, repair was uneconomic and poor old NXN6 went to the breaker's yard.

The Javelin was a memorable car to own, probably like your first kiss in my case. The design was ahead of its day and it had some character. It set me off owning larger cars, although when I saw one again about five years ago it was smaller than I remembered, a bit like places revisited from childhood!

It was good to be informed that the make still has its enthusiasts; you never know, I may join your ranks in retirement so as to complete the circle.

John Gilmore ... Lymm, Cheshire, February 1996

WET PLUGS AND BLOWN HEAD GASKETS

Further to our telephone conversation some days ago, I am enclosing some notes and comments about my experiences with a Jowett Javelin:

In 1952 a friend of mine used to borrow 'Daddy's Javelin' and take a mixed bunch from college to spend some time in Cambridge on punts on the river. We were all impressed with the car as we were able to squeeze six of us in.

In 1953 another friend of mine had a Bradford van which we used to thrash around in when we were not working on the SS Jaguar that we used to race at Clubman's events.

Between 1963 and 1964 I bought a black Javelin registered ASY422, when working in Scotland, for £85. I used to drive from Glasgow to High Wycombe, Bucks, in it before the A74 had become a dual carriageway and had to carry a wet chamois leather to wash salt off the windscreen on long winter drives. The steering and front suspension would become very tight on the way back as it had to be greased every 1,000 miles.

I was once rammed by another Javelin in Glasgow when I had to brake for a dog; both cars were drivable afterwards, but it was ironic that it was another Javelin that had caused the damage.

There used to be an enthusiast in Glasgow who had several Javelins and two Jupiters, one of which was said to have been one of the Le Mans cars. [*This will, I guess, have been George Mitchell, who ran a spares scheme for Jowett owners for many year, later selling the remainder of his stock to the Jowett Car Club ... NS*]

My final drive in the car was from Glasgow to High Wycombe again; the local garage carried out some engine work of a minor nature, and made a mess of it and had to have another go to put it right. When I got down to the Border I was leaving a trail of water and it became boring to continually keep topping it up with water. A jar of Barr's resolved that immediate problem but as we drove down the M1 the engine became rough. The AA diagnosed it as 'big ends', so we left the car by a transport café and scrounged a lift to Stamford in Lincolnshire to catch a train home. All of this did not improve my wife's appreciation of the car!

Next weekend I drove back with a friend, who also had a Javelin, and took a head gasket with us (we had managed to diagnose the most probable fault as a blown head gasket over a few pints). On a cold wet morning we jacked the car up, took the wheel off, removed the head and found it was a blown gasket. So we replaced it and two hours later we were driving down the A1 again; within half an hour I was cruising at 70 mph + and it was running beautifully.

When changing the Javelin head we noticed that although the car had covered 80,000 miles, there was no wear step on either of the bores. If I remember correctly they used hard liners in the later mark 3 engines, so I am sure with correct maintenance the car could have easily covered 150,000 miles.

Many years later I was driving my Alfa Sprint and a very similar engine feel came over the car, again the AA diagnosed big end bearing failure. On this occasion, however, it was one of the carburettors was misbehaving. Obviously if a boxer engine is not performing on both sides there is considerable imbalance which fools car mechanics who are not familiar with them.

This trip down memory lane has reminded me of another Javelin memory; putting my right foot further and further down as the car lost power. I stopped and lifted the bonnet to see that a pinhole leak in the top hose sprayed hot water under pressure onto the distributor!

Years later when I was driving a JPS Ford Capri I lost a lot of water; changing the radiator did not solve the problem, but I remembered the Javelin. After some hard driving in the Capri at night, I switched off the engine and let the car cool slightly and then opened the bonnet to find a jet of steam coming out of the top hose – it was the same fault as in the Javelin!

Mike Gold ... Molesey, Surrey, February 1996

WATCH OUT FOR THAT LAMP-POST!

In response to your request in the *Telegraph* for stories about Jowett cars, these are my stories about two cars. One owned by myself, a 1949 Javelin, the other owned by my Uncle in 1927: this was a two-seater open car of 1924 vintage.

The 1924 Jowett. In 1927 my Uncle drove this car one weekend from Tisbury, a small village near Salisbury, to Oldham near Manchester, a distance of 500 miles return. He had my Grandma, his wife, and my cousin who was seven years of age at the time with him. The car was an open two-seater with 'dicky' seat at the back in the boot; it had a small flat-twin water-cooled engine. The journey there took ten hours one Friday, and on the Saturday morning my Uncle took us all to Blackpool for the day. This was with my mother, his wife and himself on the front seat, and my father and Grandmother in the dicky seat. My cousin and myself were sat on the two rear wheel arches. We were stopped by the police on the way there as they wanted to know if my Uncle had a bus driving licence! He was in fact a long-distance lorry driver which the police seemed happy enough with, as they let us carry on to Blackpool!

The 1949 Javelin. I bought this car in Newport in 1954 and had it for two years; I paid £350 for it with a three months parts and labour guarantee. It was a black car and the body and inside looked to be in very good condition. After three weeks the timing chain broke, this was replaced by the garage under guarantee. I then found the car extremely hard to start when cold. I was then told that the garage salesman should not have given me three months guarantee on the car, so I paid for an RAC engineer to examine the car. He spent a whole morning in the garage but was still unable to start the car. He told my wife that if I could get the car to his garage he would have a word with the owner, who he knew, to see if he could get the car sorted out. This I did, and they loaned me another car while mine was being worked on. Four weeks later I got the Javelin back, the engine had been completely rebuilt and the brakes had been relined. Over the next few months I covered over 4,000 miles in her.

On a straight road it would keep up a smooth 70-75 mph, but on corners and roundabouts you had to take them at about 30 mph unless you had the boot full. On a long run it would average at about 27-30 miles to the gallon.

There always seemed to be something going wrong with the car. At one time the starter motor switch would not disconnect from the battery. To stop this I had to take one of the wires off the battery, which was under the floor in front of the rear seat. Once in my haste to take the wires off the battery I pulled one of the rear door handles off!

As usual, I parked the car outside my house on a downhill slope, one day the nearside front door was not quite closed when the handbrake came off with nobody inside the car. Luckily the car only moved about two yards forward as the 'suicide door' opened and was crumpled against a concrete lamp-post, stopping the car. This made a mess of the door, but could have been much more expensive.

I did quite a lot of minor work on the car myself and found that the carburettors needed frequent adjusting and also the tappets. I finally parted with the car when the flexible oil pipe feed to the engine broke and oil went all over the outside of the engine – I was taking my daughter to hospital at the time.

The Jowett Javelin was well ahead of its time, but not a very reliable car; I think sometimes I wish I still had it, but at seventy-six do I need the trouble?

M. R. Winterbottom ... Caldicot, Gwent, February 1996

A CORNISH JAVELIN - MCV176

Jowett Appeal – *Daily Telegraph*, 17 February 1996 – My late father, Alfred Edwards, a Cornish fish merchant of Mevagissey and Newlyn, owned a Jowett Javelin from October 1950 until the spring of 1961.

The car, which I occasionally drove, was a maroon deluxe model registered NCV176 and was purchased new by my father from a dealer in Falmouth after a

This Javelin registered NCV176 was purchased new from the Jowett agents in Falmouth in October 1950 by a Cornish fish merchant called Alfred Edwards. It was a deluxe model and was painted maroon. He kept the car until 1961, trading it in against a new Morris Oxford. The car was used mainly for trips between Mevagissey and Newlyn, and for holidays and weekend travel. It was used on one occasion for a European holiday to France, Switzerland and Italy; this snowy-looking picture was taken on Mont Cenis Pass. (Edwards)

long period on a waiting list for a new car, as was normal at that time. I believe it was subject to a covenant forbidding resale within twelve months of purchase – a measure designed to prevent a 'black market' in recent second-hand cars which at the time were in short supply.

I remember it as a stylish and comfortable car with a bench seat in the front and central armrests on the front and rear seats. It had a four-speed column-mounted gear change with a knob protruding from the end of the lever which had to be depressed to engage reverse.

The car was used regularly over the period of over ten years during my father's ownership, though the total mileage was not enormous – under 100,000 miles by the time it was traded in. It was taken back by the original Falmouth dealer in part exchange for a new Morris Oxford, as Jowett ceased production of all models in 1954. It was used mainly for journeys between Mevagissey and Newlyn and between Mevagissey and Plymouth, with occasional trips to London and a trip abroad to France, Switzerland and Italy.

For this excursion into Europe it was carried across the Channel on the Townsend ferry *Halladale* – cars were loaded, I remember, in those days, by being reversed onto the car deck by a member of the crew. The final stage of the journey to Genoa in Italy involved crossing the Lautaret and Mont Cenis passes in the Alps during an early April snowfall, which made driving difficult.

The car coped well most of the time, but did have problems sometimes. Early in its life it showed a tendency to misfire and even cut out in wet conditions, due, I believe, to the positioning of the plugs and leads close to the ground in the 'flat four' engine. This was cured, eventually, I seem to remember, by fitting some kind of rubber screening or protective device, though I don't know the details. My father always complained that the plugs were not easy to get at. Later in its life there were problems arising from corrosion in the radiator. Apart from these things I believe it was a reliable car and it was certainly pleasant to drive and its performance was good for its day.

I am afraid that I have no information as to what happened to the car after 1961, but I hope that these recollections are of interest to you.

Peter Edwards … Poulton-le-Fylde, Lancashire, February 1996

A JOWETT LOVE AFFAIR – JAVELIN OKE588

In 1959, as a married man with two children, I was stationed to Birkenhead as a Royal Marines Sergeant. There was a dire need for transport as my home was then on the Wirral and my place of work at Morpeth Dock. I purchased a Singer Super Ten from the manager of the local Midland Bank, using a loan provided by his Bank. Taking it to the local garage I reversed into their plate glass window due to brake failure. This was repaired and my family travelled to Kent to visit my wife's Aunties in Chatham where I offered one of the Aunties a lift to hospital on a routine check up when the hand-brake cable snapped on a severe slope leading to a major road (then the A2 to Dover).

Dismayed at my luck I managed to get as far as Ball's Garage in Gillingham where the earliest repairs could be carried out would have been in three days hence. By that time I was required back on duty at Birkenhead. Their salesman offered to part exchange the car against any of their stock, so at that time I became the proud owner of a Jowett Javelin.

The deal concluded (at some loss to myself) we returned home in style – real leather front and rear bench seats, column-change gear lever, superb handling, excellent power available, spacious boot space with that elongated, streamlined boot and paintwork in Goodwood (Racing) Green. Once home I 'T' cut the paint and chrome work using Brasso (military supply) and applied waxed polish throughout courtesy of the CO's Staff Car driver.

I now had the first 'flying machine' of my life, a most reliable car that gave us many hours of happy motoring, and some 30,000 miles of saloon comfort. It was spacious enough to take four adults, two children, their cat and luggage to suit all needs.

Not being 'technically minded' I could not give you much information on its specifications except to say it had a flat-four engine, in aluminium I believe, with a matching gearbox. It had good accessibility except for changing the plugs, where it was easier to remove the front wheels than 'fiddle'. Once we ran through deep water outside Birmingham which killed the engine instantly due to water resting in the plug recesses, this proved to be the car's only disadvantage.

At a later date it was apparent that a new gearbox was required. I took the car to Messrs Addison's, who were the local Jowett agent/dealers, who informed me that Jowetts were no longer in production (and had not been for some time), but spares were not a problem as a source was guaranteed for ten years up to 1964. I paid a total of £66 for the replacement and fitting. What would that cost today I wonder? This was the only repair I ever required in the time that I owned the Javelin. Servicing was 'perks' courtesy of our resident Vehicle Mechanic who drooled over the car like any Rolls-Royce owner would over his first acquisition.

I could drive at 100 miles an hour when I travelled on the newly opened M1 to Kent [*These speedo gauges were always renowned for being very optimistic! I think 85 mph is much more realistic, but still a good speed for 1961... NS*], yet in town it was so easy to park and handle. I enjoyed every minute of my time spent with that car and regret that an overseas posting in March 1962 forced us to part. Although I had offers for the car from associates in the RMs I sold it privately, but for much less than the £365 I paid for it initially.

Another memory of the car that has just come to mind was travelling to Kent on my own one Saturday afternoon in winter. I listened to the in-car radio to the sports results and around 7 p.m. was travelling down the A2 to Dartford – so far seeing nothing of the severe weather that the radio had stated was occurring in the South – then I dipped over the long hill before Meopham. It was a sheet of ice from the top to the bottom. I eased the throttle, gently applied the brakes and tried to hold the nearside kerb where a smattering of snow lay and was around halfway down the hill when a Morris Minor, parked on the grass verge, raised his trafficator (those silly little orange arms that came out from between the doors) and pulled out onto the road in front of me. In trying to avoid him I spun out of control, crossed the road, and thumped into a soil bank where pipe laying was in progress. I alighted the car shaken but unhurt to find that the tow-bar had taken the 'knock'.

The rear wheels were spinning merrily over a six-foot trench, the radio was still playing and the engine was still running, with no visible damage to the car. Using the side-jacking points and timber taken from the trench I was able to lever the car high enough to place two timbers beneath the rear wheels and escape back onto the road. My return journey was undertaken with extreme caution with ten

In 1959, Mr Jarvis was a sergeant in the Royal Marines based in Birkenhead and needed reliable transport to take him there from his home in the Wirral. He bought a Singer Super Ten, which was a mechanical disaster for him. He took it for repair at a local garage, who agreed to take this in part exchange against a Javelin registered OKE588 that they had in stock. He enjoyed every minute of ownership of the Javelin covering 30,000 trouble-free miles in it. He reluctantly parted with the car in 1962 as he had an overseas posting. (Jarvis)

inches of snow on the roof by the time I reached Chatham, only to find that the North London roads were clear again. Many inquisitive eyes saw the snow on the roof before it became dislodged – ballast was no longer necessary!

Thus I conclude my love affair with Jowett Javelin cars, but for long afterwards I spotted them on the roads in the UK with envious eyes and to this day wonder what happened to OKE558. [*Sadly, I can find no record of the car so am sure it will have been scrapped many years ago ... NS*]

Al Jarvis ... Stockton-on-Tees, Cleveland, March 1996

JAVELIN MEMORIES FROM GUERNSEY – PVT983

I owned a Javelin, registration number PVT983, which I bought second-hand for £400 in 1956. I was living in Eccleshall, Staffs, at the time. I sold it to a friend when I came to live in Guernsey in 1958.

I fitted a vacuum gauge – a very useful tuning device – and a tow-bar to pull a small two-wheeled trailer with our camping equipment. I also competed in many events with the local car club, of which I was secretary. I won't extol the car's many virtues, which will be known to you, but I can tell you of the one failure that occurred.

Whilst driving at a moderate speed there was a ghastly noise from the engine, and after I had driven it carefully home I discovered that the crankshaft had broken. I stripped the engine down and took the block to the Jowett dealer in Longton to have a new crankshaft fitted. Jowett had advised me that there was a design weakness and they would provide a redesigned crankshaft. This was either at no cost or a reduced cost – I can't now be sure – but anyway I was very impressed with Jowett's responsible attitude, bearing in mind the car was over four years old and had been purchased by me second-hand!

The dealer fitted the crankshaft and I assembled the engine, taking considerable time and care, using specialist gauges etc. from the technical department of the college where I was a lecturer.

My first trip out after completion was from Eccleshall to Reading; the performance was memorable but, on arrival, I noticed oil in the exhaust pipe, and on checking the engine oil level, found it very low.

I diagnosed that when the dealer had fitted the new crankshaft he had failed to correctly seal the carburettor balance pipe at the joint between the two halves of the block and the engine was therefore sucking oil into the cylinders.

I drove carefully back to Eccleshall, keeping an eye on the oil levels, and thence to the Longton dealer. He admitted responsibility and said that if I stripped the

This Javelin registered PTV983 was bought in 1956 by Alec Forty from his local garage for £400; he was living in Eccleshall, Staffs, at the time. He ran the car for two years, but he then sold it to a friend, as he was moving to Guernsey. During his ownership, he suffered a broken crankshaft, but his garage had to rebuild the engine again, as they did not get one of the balance pipe seals in correctly. Alec fitted a tow bar to the car so that he could tow a trailer with camping equipment inside. (Forty)

engine again he'd put the seal back correctly. I argued, with some force – and successfully – that it was his responsibility to strip the engine, since it was his work that had caused the trouble.

This time he correctly sealed the balance pipe and re-assembled the engine, but the performance was nowhere as good as it had been after my assembly. I took it back to the dealer for a test drive with his works manager, who said the car's performance was perfectly correct. I argued that it was nothing like as good as it had been after I had assembled it and he said that I must have achieved a 'freak tuning'!

I sent the full story to Jowett, with the details of my work and they wrote back confirming that I had done it correctly for my Series 2 engine but the dealer had done it to Series 1 specification!

Back to the dealer, who was persuaded to tune the engine 'correctly', but it was never quite as good as that wonderful trip down to Reading. As you say in Yorkshire, 'If tha' wants owt done, do it th' sen'. With apologies for the spelling!

Well those are my recollections of a very advanced car for its day.

Alec Forty ... St Andrew, Guernsey, February 1996

A CAR SALES PERSON WITH JOHN SURTEES CONNECTIONS

Having been retired from the car sales world for over twenty years, I have had plenty of time to put my snaps into albums and write little stories about my selling of so many lovely cars.

I enclose a snap of a Jowett Javelin on my Sales front at Peckham Rye in 1953. The car looks to be very good value at £595; as you can see it is a 1952 model. I have sold almost all Jowett models over the years including the pre-war cars and vans.

During the war in 1944 I was stationed in Windrush, near Burford, and one of the officers had a Jowett Flat-Four Saloon. I did a job for him on the motor; it was a super little car.

The first time I drove a Javelin I was surprised at how fast it was considering its small engine capacity. At the time I was running a Bristol 400 and I seem to remember that the Javelin was as fast from 0-60 mph as the Bristol. The road holding and ride were also very good; above average in fact. It was such a pity that they had to cease production when they did.

This will also be of interest to your members. When John Surtees went full-time as a works rider for Norton, he no longer had to take his own machines in a van. So he bought a Jowett Jupiter and many people will remember John and his mother, Dorothy, going to many circuits in that car whilst his father, Jack, looked after the Vincent Motorcycle business in Forest Hill. I had the great pleasure of being on *This is Your Life* with John Surtees in December 1992. Cars were my business and motorcycling was my hobby – a great life!

James W. Oliver ... Weymouth, Dorset, February 1996

James Oliver's sales lot at Peckham Rye in 1953 with a 1952 Javelin deluxe registered EVG682 for sale at £595; 'a one owner car' at a typical bombsite second-hand car sales site in the mid-1950s. It looks a nice car, but sadly, it is not on the list of known survivors. (Oliver)

MEMORIES OF TWO JAVELINS AND EARLY JOWETT CAR CLUB INVOLVEMENT

I was the first secretary of the Jowett Car Club (not the Southern Jowett Car Club) which had its beginnings in about 1963, from which I resigned in about 1965. I doubt that many of the original committee members still survive. I am pleased, however, that the club is still in existence.

As secretary I organised treasure hunts, meetings and one Concours d'elegance at Chatsworth House in Derbyshire in, as I recall, 1965. I also submitted reports of our activities to the Southern Jowett Car Club, which were published in their periodical. I was somewhat surprised when reports of their activities did not include a single Jowett vehicle – strictly a club for club members!

I had two Javelins, the first was chassis number D8/PA/953, purchased in 1954 for £400, the car was by then six years of age with 29,000 miles on the clock. It was refurbished by Jowett Engineering in 1957 when a reconditioned engine, numbered RO12608, was fitted and the front suspension rebuilt. I eventually gave it away to a fellow club member (less engine) who had an engine but no car. The engine life, I found, rarely exceeded 40-45,000 miles – rear main bearing failure usually was the cause.

The second was a 1953 model which I bought in 1964, with rubberised front suspension and a stiffened crankcase, the chassis number, I believe, was 23,838. This car was a maverick which would whip into vicious oversteer without warning. I and the surviving Jowett garages could never figure out why. It did it once too often in 1966 and was written off.

Well I had Javelins from 1954 to 1966, rebuilt several engines because garages didn't want to know, which was hardly surprising since most of them didn't even know what a torque wrench was! I still have a torque wrench which I bought when the JCC went to Jowett Engineering Ltd at Howden Clough on a trip I organised in 1964 when they were closing down having fulfilled the obligation of 10 years of spares and service. If I recall correctly, I paid the princely sum of £2 10s 0d for it and it still works perfectly on the odd occasion I need to use it.

I recall during a visit to Idle I saw the 'new' Jowett saloon, which I thought was a great cumbersome-looking thing, very similar to the then Singer 1500. I don't believe it was ever marketed. [*This will have been the CD saloon, only one of which was made along with one pick-up and about a dozen estate cars and vans. The car was abandoned at the back of the buildings at Howden Clough after closure in 1964, so sadly scrapped. The pick-up was also scrapped at a later date. One CD Estate still survives in the UK and is undergoing a full restoration ... NS*]

At the time of the closure of the factory in 1954 they had been developing a new sports car, again ahead of its time, with a fibreglass body on a new chassis, known as the R4 Jupiter. Only three of these R4s were produced, and I could never trace what happened to them. [*Two of them still exist ... NS*]

I also tried to buy a special-bodied Jupiter in about 1960, which had been commissioned from a specialist builder in, or about, Coventry. I was told that it took three years to build, and apart from the radiator grille, it was pure Jaguar E Type FHC. The garage (Holden & Hastings of Burnley) couldn't do a deal so it fell through but I often wonder what happened to that car. I only know that the chap who finally bought it had three crankshaft failures in no time at all! Strangely enough I drove Javelins for well over 100,000 miles and never had a broken crank – a fault that plagued the engine until the oval web crank was introduced. Happy days!

Don March ... West Bradford, Clitheroe, Lancashire, February 1996

JAVELIN LYA576

Re our Javelin LYA576, it was bought new by my father from the Jowett agents Sparrow's in Yeovil, Somerset, all bright and new; the colour was metallic turquoise blue. My father's name was C. D. Sweet, and his address at that time was 'Dentworth' Over Stratton, South Petherton, Somerset. It was unfortunately damaged three weeks after we took delivery of the car (July 1949) and was returned to Jowett's at Idle for repair. In 1955 or early 1956 my father had the Javelin sprayed black as the original colour had faded.

When my parents, my husband and myself visited France in August 1957 we went over in the Javelin and had an enjoyable touring holiday. We also went to

Andorra in the car before the roads were properly made up and it was quite a climb. We passed several cars who were boiling but the Javy just sailed past with no problems at all. Later in the holiday, however, we had to change the front wheel bearing. My father had taken various spares with us and my husband and father spent one night replacing the bearing! There was much horn blowing when we were returning through France, as we had spotted a Javelin coming in the other direction. We crossed the Channel by plane – the Silver City Service from Southampton to Cherbourg.

We had a second Javelin which was registered NFJ799; we bought it in 1963 and it was a 1953 example that had been first registered in Exeter. It was bought from Henry Bowers in Chard, Somerset; he was an agricultural engineer and just sold cars as a sideline. I am sorry that I have no pictures of this car, they must have been lost in the three moves we have had since.

Mrs Betty Lomax … Dawlish, Devon, March 1996

TRUE TALES OF JOWETT JAVELIN OWNERSHIP IN NIGERIA

I had received a letter from Keith Nixon, who was now living in Guernsey, but at the time of his Javelin ownership he was living in Nigeria, Africa. He had various mechanical problems with the car, of which I asked him for more details. This superb letter is his reply to me.

The oil pressure warning light on my 1951 Javelin was situated just above the front passenger's right knee. It was about the size of a grain of rice and its feeble light did not show up in Africa's midday sun. The first hint that I had lost the sump plug was the sound of mice under the bonnet. I stopped the car on the dirt track road, lifted the bonnet and removed a hot, dry dipstick. Looking under the front bumper oil was still dripping from the sump and the centre ridge of the roads which was only about three inches. It was Easter weekend 1952 and I was treating my three friends to a picnic on the edge of the Plateau in Nigeria, three thousand feet up and over three thousand miles south of Bradford! Fortunately I had run the car in carefully in England and only collected it from Lagos in March.

We decided to split up – the married couple would walk ahead seeking signs of civilisation whilst the other bachelor would walk with me looking for the sump plug on the rutted bush track. At least we were not worried by passing traffic, as herds of white cattle outnumbered the cars. We never found the sump plug but about an hour later my friends arrived in a pick-up truck; they had brought with them a can of clean oil, a sharp knife and a piece of wood. The wood was whittled down to fit, driven into the drain hole with a stone; and a gallon of cold oil was poured into the engine. It started straight away and after congratulations all round we set off back for home some forty miles away. Very gradually I relaxed, thinking we had got away with it.

A light tapping sound came a few days later. We all worked at a veterinary research centre so it was easy to lay my hands on a stethoscope. The diagnosis was a damaged big end and bearing, and most likely the front one. My neighbour said that changing the big ends was the sort of job you do at the side of the road – 'So how about doing it next Sunday?'

Much later I discovered that he had lost his two front teeth when a big end cap fell on them! Fortunately the nearby 'Sleeping Sickness Research Lab' had a ramp for servicing lorries, a six-foot working height and storage space for 44-gallon drums of oil. It was roofed in but lacked electric power, so we removed the sump and beat out the dent, carefully unfastened the locking tabs and big end tabs and found perfectly polished bearings. The good news was that they didn't need replacing; the bad news was that the noise may have come from the main bearing. I was told that all engines made strange noises but nobody knew what the flat-four Jowett should sound like, but they came to listen and offer their opinions!

The light noise continued and the diagnosis was as we say guarded: 'Get a set of main bearings and a workshop manual and have a look.' This I did, but the instructions were quite brief: 'To gain access to the main bearings it is necessary to remove the engine, clutch and gearbox from the frame.'

The cradle to support the engine was made from an old fence post and two blocks of mahogany. I narrowly escaped injury when the earth floor of the garage collapsed and the jack fell into a termite tunnel, but I managed to scramble clear, ripping my shirt on the jacking pillar. So we decided we needed to move the car nearer to the back door of my bungalow and pray for a dry day. I disconnected everything, supported the engine on the cradle I made and we pushed the car away, allowing the engine to emerge through the front grille. We now had the engine, clutch and gearbox on a jack at the bottom of a short flight of steps leading to my bathroom. How did we get it under cover and to a working height? Adamu Vom! Adamu was a cattle attendant who could take a young bull by the horns and wrestle it to the ground and pin it upside down by its pointed horns. He could run with a 2 cwt sack of corn on his shoulders. We showed him the two-inch-thick mahogany table in the bathroom and asked him if he could lift the engine from the front of the Javelin and carry it up the steps and put it on the table. He seemed very happy with the shilling we gave him, which was a day's wages for him.

So we now had the whole works indoors with electricity and warm water to hand. I took a bath and contemplated the problems ahead, as nobody here had stripped a Jowett engine before and spares were limited to the Continental touring kit I bought with the car. So I was now going to have to share my bathroom with the Javelin engine, so while I waited for the parts to arrive from Bradford I had a look at the valves. I did a de-coke and skimmed the exhaust valves on an ML7 lathe. By Whit Sunday the engine was back in the car and our Ford-trained mechanic offered to set the ignition spot on with his Avometer. When I came to collect it at the end of his working day he screwed his face up like a lemon. He didn't know what he had done to it, but thought it might still be of use to potter about in locally about the station. It was a huge disappointment – my first new car had cost me a year's salary and after six weeks work it was ruined! So I forgot about lunch and got the workshop manual and looked up ignition timing. Using a piece of cigarette paper between the points and the flywheel markings, I reset it myself. I was delighted as the performance was restored; I took the Ford man for a run – he was amazed. He had set it to TDC and then advanced it until it pinked – but it never did!

The Javelin had to be serviced every five hundred miles, but I lived so far away from Lagos the car was due another oil change by the time I got back home.

My mechanically minded neighbour suggested that the few steps leading to his veranda were a danger and that they needed a low wall to prevent people falling. By building the walls the same distance apart as the wheel track he could then drive up a ramp onto the veranda and service his car by sitting in a storm drain under the eaves. When he left for Kenya I took over his bungalow – but found I wasn't alone. Near the back door, in a dimly lit passage he had left a dry chamois leather screwed up. When I opened the door the chamois moved – it was a small female bat with a jellybaby-sized baby locked onto a nipple. Very carefully I scooped it up and hung it by its two thumbs on an outside wall. It took off again in daylight, the baby bat swinging like a pendulum and with spectacular precision the adult bat folded its wings around the youngster and both shot under my corrugated iron roof. The designer of aircraft undercarriage doors must have copied it.

On my next leave I called at Idle and discussed the odd intermittent tapping noises. A sympathetic engineer came back with a small spring, like a heavy-duty lighter spring. This feeble device was to control camshaft end float, but it was not man enough for the task. What I needed was a cross cut into the head of a bolt screwed through the timing case cover, held by a lock nut and adjusted to just clear the camshaft, then locked in place. He gave me a bolt and explained how to fit it – when I did the noise vanished!

So was all my work a waste of time or not? Not at all. When I returned to England I took the car on its fifth birthday back to Idle and booked it in for a full overhaul. I could talk to engineers who recognised an enthusiast. Would I like them to fit a Jupiter crankshaft? If they assembled it tight would I obey the running in instructions?

If you saw a Tampico Beige Javelin creeping along at 30 miles an hour in July 1956 it was me! I sold it at auction in Lancaster in 1958 for £285 cash. We still talk about the Javelin forty years on – my first new car.

Keith Nixon ... Castel, Guernsey, March 1996

THE HISTORY OF JAVELIN LOP711

I bought the above registered Javelin in 1960. The original log book (which I still have) confirms the date of my acquisition as being 10 November 1960. The original colour was beige but the log book shows that it was repainted light grey in 1959 and again to light blue in October 1960. The engine and chassis numbers were both E1/PC/18972/D which confirms the original engine was still in the car.

The first owners of the car were the Jowett agents, Hyde's (Birmingham) Ltd; they used the car until 13 January 1952 when it was sold to an owner in Leicester, and there were another five changes prior to me buying the car, so I was its eighth owner.

I seem to remember paying £85 for the car, which was not in prime condition, but adequate for my purpose. I regret that I cannot remember the odometer reading at the time of my purchase. After giving the car a thorough servicing, as was my custom, I was impressed with the road holding, steering and acceleration, although the brakes, I seem to remember, took some sorting out.

Initial problems in service centred round the unreliability of the ignition system in wet conditions, which was overcome by filling the plug caps with silicone grease. Also the constant movements in the rear supports for the cooling fan bearing housing, which was never satisfactorily fixed – it was just necessary to keep a spare in the car at all times.

On the road the car was fast (90 mph + was indicated on the odometer), relatively economical (about 35 mpg, not bad for a 1500cc engine of the time with twin carburettors), comfortable on long journeys (my wife was always impressed), and in my opinion have only had one more comfortable car – a Citroën GS, but that was almost twenty years later! It was also a good load carrier; I remember one journey of 50 miles with six burly RAF officers plus myself travelling to a dinner invitation.

However, maintaining the vehicle was something else. The water jacket core plugs were a nightmare because of cylinder block corrosion in the counter bores (I finished up by drilling and tapping the adjacent faces and bolting ¼-inch plates, well gasketted, to the faces); heavy crankcase breathing and high oil consumption (which necessitated engine removal twice, first to change piston rings and bearing shells, and the second to fit what was said to be one of the last oval web crankshafts available in the London area – this overcame the problem). Also jumping (no – leaping) out of gear in the indirect ratios – which necessitated a third engine removal.

Worst of all was while out with the family one day, on rounding a fairly sharp bend in a country lane, there was a very loud bang from somewhere beneath the driver's seat. Nothing was obvious on cursory inspection, so the car was driven home where, on a flat surface, it was seen that there was a decided list to starboard. Closer inspection revealed that the chassis, formed of deep and shallow channel sectioned stampings, spot welded along their flanges, had failed at the spot welds along the top, due to the twisting effect derived from the offside front torsion bar, the anchorage for which was bolted to the shallow channel section, plus, undoubtedly, a modicum of corrosion. After a lot of head scratching, this was fixed by bolting a large load spreader made of 18 inches of 4½ channel section girder, drilling through the girder and both chassis members and inserting 2-inch x ¼-inch U-bolts, about 6 inches long around the front and rear of the torsion bar anchorage point and then tightening the U-bolts to bring the shallow chassis member back to its original position. This lasted for the remaining life of the car – about eighteen months.

For the last six months of the life of the car, it was in the hands of a colleague, while I was on aircraft trials in Libya. Upon my return he told me with some amusement that he had had some trouble with the windscreen wipers, and that upon taking the cover off the gearbox of the wiper motor, he had found the casing fully packed with white grease – the sort used in those days for brake cam and cable lubrication!

The log book tells me that it was licensed up to the end of September 1962, which was slightly later than the date of my return from Libya. I was faced with a problem – the impending instruction of the MOT inspection requirement meant that it would have been highly unlikely to have passed any reasonable testing station at that time, and my conscience did not allow me to sell it in that condition, and I am sure no one would have bought it if they were appraised of the 'modification', so the car was reluctantly broken up. Again, I have no recollection of the odometer reading at that time, although my average annual mileage in those days was about 18,000-20,000.

In breaking the car, I found that I had done the right thing since, firstly, the condition of the corrosion and spot welds on the chassis had worsened since the original assessment and, secondly, the steering box was found to be in an advanced state of failure as one of the securing lugs was found to be completely separated from the housing, and the second was partially cracked through. It seems that, in spite of my earlier observation that the steering was good. The steering column was only held in place at its lower end by the restraining effect of the floorboards! The body and chassis were disposed of at the local tip and the engines (I had acquired a second as a spare, just in case!) and transmission components were sold to Javelin-owning colleagues, which brought in about £50, so not a bad outcome.

Shortly before my departure to Libya, the car had been crunched on the rear offside door by a careless parker, so I ordered from my friendly spares stockist in Harrow a replacement door skin, which if I remember correctly, cost me £2 or £3. Because I broke the car the skin was never used and is in my loft along with a maintenance manual and a spare parts list for the car. I also have some parts in my garage, for example, the fuel tank has served as a storage container for kerosene for many years, and I know that the ignition/lighting switch is still here somewhere.

I look back with mixed emotions to this vehicle and the friendliness which went with it – you could always expect a wave from a passing Javelin.

For the sake of interest, I should say that my father, long since deceased, used a Bradford van from circa 1947 to 1952 in his capacity as a television service engineer. The vehicle gave him reliable service apart from, as I can remember, some trouble with corrosion of the induction manifold due to its proximity to the engine coolant. Beyond that, I regret that I cannot remember any further details.

Stan Haselton ... Abbots Langley, Herts, February 1996

JAVELIN SX7666

I am a seventy-nine-year-old retired engineer and I can confirm I owned a 1952 deluxe Javelin for approximately eleven years. As you can see from the enclosed copy invoice, I paid £465 for her on 25 May 1955 and that the car was registered SX7666; I am sure this invoice will be of interest to your members.

While I owned the Javelin my wife and I decided we would like to try caravanning. In order to get the correct fixing points for my tow bar I wrote to Jowett's asking them for their advice. This resulted in them sending me a complete set of drawings for the installation of a tow bar. I am enclosing these for you in the original envelope they arrived in. [*Now in the club archive ... NS*]

My own experiences of the Javelin was that its road holding was very good, the steering was accurate and did not produce much feedback through the steering wheel. The brakes never left me with any problems even when I was towing a caravan with the car.

The column gear change was recognised by many as the best ever produced. I certainly never had any problems disengaging any gear, and the travel from gear to gear was quite short and positive.

One real trouble I experienced with the car on a regular basis was that the ignition would 'drown' in heavy rain and wet roads. I tried all kinds of ways to reduce this problem, but never succeeded in protecting it fully.

Possibly the greatest trouble I had with the car was a broken crankshaft, this took place only three miles from my home. I stopped the car because of the abnormal noise, but the engine was still running. I suspected that the noise was coming from the front of the engine. On removing the plug lead from plug number 1 the noise was greatly reduced, so I then removed the plug and drove very slowly home on the remaining three cylinders.

Until the engine was removed and stripped down I had no suspicion that the crankshaft had broken. The break had taken place on the web between number 1 and 2 cylinders, number 1 piston and valve gear was still being driven in spite of the fracture. By removing the spark plug I had removed all the load from the crankshaft journal of number 1 cylinder, and the only torque required to drive the valve gear was being transmitted through the crack in the web.

By the time this occurred spares were rather scarce and I could not find a replacement. At this time I was employed as Chief Maintenance Engineer in a rather large factory and had access to the necessary machine tools to produce a replacement. A piece of Nickel Chrome Molybdenum steel was acquired and this was machined all over leaving approx +0.10 inches on the journals and sent for Nitrate casehardening to a depth of 0.025 inches; it was then sent to specialist crankshaft grinders for grinding and balancing.

When I finally sold the car in 1968 the crankshaft was still in the car and must have covered over 30,000 miles.

I do hope that this small amount of information that I have gathered over the years will now be kept by the Jowett Car Club for posterity. [*Yes, it has – many thanks ... NS*]

Daniel B. Hart ... Rutherglen, Glasgow, May 1996

PLENTY OF FAULTS WITH THIS JAVELIN!

My father purchased a black Jowett Javelin saloon in approximately 1952. It was a very advanced car for that time; it was economical, fast and stylish with its sloping back. Comfort and ride was good and the interior was very well finished with a wood-grained dashboard and hinged glove box pockets. The road holding was excellent due to the engine layout well forward and slung between the front wheels.

My father was not a chap who would hang about when he was driving. He was always in a hurry and I remember him on several occasions priding himself on the fact that he had reached 90 mph in the car again. Those were the good points about the car, now here are the bad ones.

In icy conditions the car was lethal, being heavy on the front and very light on the back end. We once did a complete U-turn in the car in front of a double-decker bus, only managing to miss it by mounting the pavement, ending up broadsides in front of it.

It was probably his driving, but my father was continually complaining about the tyre wear on the front wheels. I don't think the tyres of those days were up to the performance of the car.

The unique design of the car with its flat-four horizontally opposed engine made access to the plugs very difficult. In fact, he found it easier to remove the front wheel when work in that area was required.

Another problem, which was the same as the early Minis, was that the engine suffered when driving in heavy rain where the roads were wet, the exposed electrics suffered misfires.

The biggest problem we encountered, however, was with the gearbox; as you are no doubt aware it was a steering column gear change four-speed box. First gear was engaged by bringing the gear lever towards you and then straight up. For reverse it was a similar position but was engaged by pressing the knob on the end of the gear lever in. On several occasions my father engaged first gear and pressed the button at the same time, so jamming the car in first gear. All he could do then was limp round to the garage in first gear to get them to disengage it for him again.

My father eventually changed it for a new Ford Zephyr, a six-cylinder job, a different car altogether, but the interior was not as good as the Javelin.

Regarding Bradford vans, a friend of my father's purchased one from the same local Jowett dealer, it had a flat-twin engine and it always had a strange-sounding tick-over, but this chap thought the world of it. He later fitted side windows and fitted rear seats, converting it into an estate car. [*This was common practice at this time, as purchase tax was not charged on new vans. If windows were fitted at a later date the tax was avoided ... NS*]

The last time that I used my father's Javelin was when I was at college and my father let me use it to take my stuff back to my digs. I was looking forward to a high-speed 120-mile trip, but unfortunately the clutch gave out and I had to be towed home again; that will have been in 1954, and if I recall correctly it was part-exchanged for the Ford very soon after.

Brian Salisbury ... Honiton, Devon, February 1996

THE BRIEF OWNER OF TWO JAVELINS

My first Javelin was originally owned by my brother, who sadly died last year. He sold it to me in 1961 for £175. It was light green in colour. I was very proud of this car, which was registered KOF757. It was a superb car. It was the second car that I had owned and was a big step up from my first car, a pre-war Morris Ten with large running boards. Sadly my ownership of this Javelin was short-lived, as it was written-off by a huge American Plymouth Sedan, the driver of which lost control of it and hit me broadside on. The Javelin's strength stood up well to the impact and both drivers survived – hence I am writing this account to you now. I did, however, manage to break the plastic steering wheel with my head, which required some stitches in afterwards.

Sadly that was the end of a beautiful motor, which had to be replaced by another Javelin, the new one being registered DST253 and painted in two-tone black and white. Old paperwork I still have says I bought this car on 17 February 1962, and the first year's motor insurance was £1.50, which must have been a good deal! I ran this car for about a year before trading it in for a Wolseley 9/90 automatic. So my Jowett ownership was short and sweet.

I still think that Javelins were well ahead of their time, and with some updating would still sell well today. I particularly remember the smooth flat-four engine, the

Clive Pether's pride and joy was his first Javelin registered KOF757. Sadly, his ownership of it was short-lived, as it was written-off by a huge American Plymouth saloon, the driver of which lost control of it and hit him broadside on. The Javelin's strength stood up well to the impact and both drivers survived! (Pether)

handle winder for the front bench seat for aft and height and also the picnic shelf which fitted into the back of the front seat with two sockets; so easy and simple but very practical.

Clive Pether ... Paignton, Devon, January 2002

JAVELIN MKC1 AND OTHERS

The father of one of the apprentices at my college who was a draughtsman with Alfred Holt & Co., a prominent shipping company in Liverpool, owned a Javelin. We very occasionally had the use of his car, and partly as a result of this I bought another Javelin from a local dealer and enthusiast, Brian Baker, in Crowborough, soon after I eventually left for sea in 1965.

I paid, I think, £40 for this car which was a black standard model registered LDF738. It was a good runner and carried me regularly to work and back, about eighty miles a day for about eighteen months, as well as holidays in Cornwall and local travel. I also entered it in many car rallies including the National and International Jowett rallies; in fact I still have my trophy board. Eventually, however, it developed metal fatigue in the area of the trunnion brackets on the front suspension – I never saw this problem anywhere else on any other Javelin in over twenty years. I asked Brian if he knew of any others going, and he pointed me to a black deluxe model which was about to be scrapped in Lancing, West Sussex. It was in quite good condition, although the back bumper had been caught on the owner's gatepost and was badly bent, and the crankshaft was broken, it was chassis number E2/PD/21105/D and registered MKC1.

I think I paid £10 for the car; I changed the engines over, eventually rebuilding the original one with an oval web crankshaft and refitting it. I dismantled LDF738 for spares, only the body shell eventually being left. I kept all the other parts, and they were eventually sold in 1987 with MKC1 together with loads of other spares which just seemed to have just 'arrived' – more about this later.

I eventually traced the history of this car: it had been first registered in Liverpool and still had the garage plate 'Carr's Motors, Hardman Street, Liverpool' fitted on the glove compartment lid. It looks like it had been sat in the showroom for several months before being sold to Admiral Sir Max Horton, the man given the task by Churchill of defeating the U-boat menace. I believe the Admiral died only a few weeks after taking delivery of the car. The car remained in the same family as it was next registered to his daughter, surname by then Ewing-Horton, about eighteen months later.

The car found its way to the South Coast, where it was regularly serviced by the Jowett agents Marriott's Garage, Lancing. It was seen and admired there by the next owner who bought it from Mrs Ewing-Horton (I don't recall the date), who was by then living in Hove. I met this man at a 'Lost Causes of Motoring' rally at Beaulieu in the mid-1960s (again I forget his name). It was pouring with rain and this bedraggled figure came up to the car, banged on the window and shouted, 'I used to own that car!' He told me about the previous owners, and that he in turn sold it to a neighbour in Lancing whose son had used it to go to college. It was his son who damaged the bumper and broke the crankshaft.

I continued to 'rally' the car throughout the summer months all over southern England, and joined the Jowett Car Club, serving on the Southern Committee for some time (not the Southern Jowett Car Club) – I still have the enamelled bumper badge. In 1969, my fiancée and I were saving to buy a house; one evening the phone rang and a Mr Michael Keith Coburn, owner of a nightclub in Birkenhead and the Llangollen Bridge Hotel, asked to buy the car. He really only wanted the number plate so I agreed to sell this for £200, which gave us the deposit for our house in Eastbourne. The car, which I kept, was issued with a replacement registration number, 6469TU; we bought the house and were married in March 1970.

I soon had a job with a Company car (Ford Anglia van actually), and so we used the Javelin as daily private transport. My wife then bought a Triumph Vitesse registered 1001JG, which she used regularly until she was expecting our daughter and could not get behind the steering wheel comfortably. The chassis was in a dreadful state, beyond my means to restore, so she then reverted to using the Javelin (lots of room and light to drive).

During the next sixteen years this car was our daily transport, taking us and our two children on holidays and lots of outings all over the place – we love picnics – like the New Forest, Cheddar Gorge, and on one memorable occasion, to Blackpool and back in one night. We clocked up about 120,000 miles before a series of major body and chassis repairs combined with the need for a full set of new tyres at about £80 each meant we had to lay the car up. We sold it in 1987 to an electrician in Hastings together with all the spares accumulated over the years. These included five engines (one dismantled), seven gearboxes, one back axle, four radiators, two sets of upholstery, a set of doors and a boot and bonnet. It took him three Ford P100 loads to shift it all.

There are a lot of stories in between, including a trip to George Mitchell's at Cleish when, during a touring holiday in Scotland, I managed to put a hole in the sump on a switchback road between Coatbridge and Tomintoul; the time a piston broke and I drove home like James Bond followed by a smokescreen (it happened again about a month later); and the day my wife and young daughter had to walk about half a mile to Grandma's house after a wheel rim split and let the inner tube out!

For your records I can tell you the fate of another Javelin, this was registered DJG10, chassis number 414, it was rescued from an orchard at Plumpton in Sussex and dismantled at the time of the Aberfan disaster.

Ian P. Howell ... Eastbourne, East Sussex, May 1996

JAVELIN REGISTERED HHM986

I bought my Javelin registered HHM986 in Ashford, Kent, in about 1967 and used it on a regular basis; the enclosed photo was taken at Great Yarmouth in 1969. Although I had problems keeping it running as the only family transport, it has become the car that gave me most pleasure of all the cars I have owned. It was around 1972 that I could no longer keep the car, as at the time, I was not able to afford to run a second car, so I sold it to Bill Jackson who was the Suffolk area secretary of the Jowett Car Club. At the time I think he lived in Claire or Cavendish near Sudbury, Suffolk.

I took the car to the JCC Rally in Beaulieu in 1970; I remember that the whole weekend was sunny and warm, an ideal setting and I thoroughly enjoyed it. More so because I found out for the first time how helpful people could be towards a fellow enthusiast in distress. About three miles from the rally site HHM stopped firing completely. Within twenty minutes I was joined by a Javelin, Jupiter and traction engine. We eventually found that the distributor drive shaft had broken off at the bottom, so I was towed the remaining distance by the traction engine.

There were far too many cooks fixing the problem, someone had a spare shaft and five experts converged to take control of the job. There was no charge for the shaft and I couldn't get close enough to get my hands dirty, such was their enthusiasm to help. Anyway, after a great weekend my journey back to Great Yarmouth was uneventful (I had moved there in 1968). This was the longest journey I did in the Javelin.

The other photo is the Farr-bodied Jupiter, which I told you about. This was probably the biggest motoring mistake of my life when I sold it in about 1976, because I no longer had anywhere to store it. From memory I am sure its registration number was MTJ300, but I have nothing to back that up with, as although I took plenty of photos of it, I have none left showing its registration number.

Jeff Kendall ... Great Yarmouth, Norfolk, February 1993

MTJ300 is still alive and well and is now owned by the JCC member Sheila Rigg; it was given to her by her father, Frank Cooke, who was also the club treasurer in the 1980s. MTJ300 was the first of four special-bodied Jupiters built by J. E. Farr of Blackburn, Lancs. This car was built for R. Ellison and was his entry for the 1952 Monte Carlo Rally. The car crashed at Le Puy and had to be dragged out of a ravine by a team of oxen. The car went on to finish the rally, but was not an official finisher, as it was a day late.

VINTAGE AND JAVELIN MEMORIES

My first acquaintance was with a 1926 fabric-bodied saloon with a push-up air vent which was about 6 or 8 inches square on the roof. It was fitted with artillery wheels and had the usual Jowett flat-twin engine. Anyway my Dad bought it almost new and I remember reading one of the sales slogans, 'Has the pull of an elephant and the appetite of a canary.' They were right; it would go just about anywhere and was very economical on fuel.

I was given 4d for polishing the radiator with Brasso and painting the fabric roof with linseed oil as required. I learned to drive in this old faithful car of ours. However, Dad part exchanged it in 1936 for a newer faster Ford (the old girl was a bit slow). Dad was sorry he let her go after all the reliable service it had given us.

Many years later, 1955 in fact, I was sent to Nyasaland as a group engineer for a large tea estate – incidentally it is called Malawi nowadays. While there I bought one of the last Javelins off the production line. Due to its independent suspension it gave me good service on dirt roads through the tea estates. I liked the advanced design in that the tie rod ends that were adjustable and drive shaft couplings that were flexible rubber fabric and never wore out like cv joints. The downside was the way the plugs were quickly filled with water when it rained. I tried all manner of things to deflect the water away from the cylinder heads, but it was a persistent problem. I also had to fit a 1/8-inch-thick steel plate as a sump protector to be able to drive through Mozambique (Portuguese East Africa) because the only road through was like driving along a stony riverbed, in fact the only time you knew you were on the right road was seeing the telephone wire poles ahead of you. If they were not visible, I used a compass which I always carried with me. It was also possible to see the odd lion, giraffe or elephant passing through the bush on either side of the 'road'. But throughout it all, the Javelin never missed a beat – while it did not rain! And fortunately it didn't.

I packed up my job in Malawi because of my wife's health, and opened up a garage and general engineering business in Salisbury, taking my Javelin with me where it was much admired, and more than a few of my customers wanted me to sell it to them. One of them owned a new Triumph TR2; anyway, I was driving back from Salisbury after doing some shopping along the Golden Sands Road. It is a long slow drop of 2,000 feet in 20 miles and the TR2 owner came alongside and he said, 'Let's see if your Javelin can do the ton!' Well I had never had her flat out, and I knew it was not designed to do 'the ton', but I thought why not, so I put my foot down and watched the needle creep up to 94 mph, which was not bad for a 1.5-litre saloon. However, this feeling of happiness was about to end, as I had to brake hard due to goats being on the road. This resulted in clouds of blue smoke from the exhaust which, on investigation, proved to be one of the 'O' ring seals on the end of the carburettor balance pipe through the crankcase being sucked off its seating, hence all the smoke.

I took the engine out, split the crankcase, removed the balance pipe and blocked off the balance pipe breathing holes in each head. I then removed the carburettors and fabricated two spacer pedestals and passed a new balance pipe over the outside of the crankcase. After that I never had any further trouble with seals bursting.

Well I guess that is all I can tell you about the Jowetts in my life. I did eventually sell the Javelin in 1964, but the person who bought it had it stolen and it was never recovered.

A. Kay ... Lea, Preston, February 1996

JAVELIN IN NEW ZEALAND

I bought a Jowett Javelin in May or June 1952 and was able to leapfrog the waiting list to buy a new car by virtue of the fact of imminently moving to New Zealand. So the Javelin became an 'export model' as Jowett was one of the few manufacturers who were not totally absorbed in 'dollar sales' so I went to their showroom off Piccadilly (Albemarle Street) and ordered one. It was coloured Athena Grey with red leather upholstery. When the car was ready I travelled up to Bradford and picked it up from the Jowett factory and paid for it there.

The new price was £1,275, which was the same price as a Mk5 Jaguar, but as I had to pay no UK taxes my bill was for £700 plus £70 for shipment.

The Javelin was a beautifully made car in every respect and in my two years of driving in New Zealand, I had no trouble whatsoever. When my time came to return to the UK, I sold the car to a New Zealand main Jowett dealer for £900 after paying about £120 import duty.

There was no severe frost problem in New Zealand and so no salt was spread on the roads. It is not impossible, therefore, to think that the Javelin may have survived!

I had to own four other cars before I had one in the same class as the Javelin; that was an early example of the Jaguar Mk2 2.4.

John Pope ... Stone, Aylesbury, Bucks, February 1996

A SCOTTISH JAVELIN

Whilst living in Thurso, Caithness, in 1960, I bought a 1952 Javelin saloon with an 'SH' registration in Glasgow. The car was silver with red leather trim. [*Athena Grey ... NS*]

However, during the drive home from Glasgow I soon realised that the engine was not up to scratch. My first examination revealed a cracked cylinder head, which the dealer replaced, however I decided there and then to remove and strip the engine (all to be done in a lock-up type garage!).

From memory I recall having the camshaft journals metal resprayed and ground oversize so that I could hand scrape and remove the ovality from the casing bearings. This was tedious but rewarding. During the rebuild I fitted a new oval web crankshaft and bearings, new wet liners and pistons plus valves and guides. Before refitting the engine I removed the front off-side torsion bar in order to weld the rear socket to the chassis.

On completion the car performed very well and I ran it for a number of years before selling it locally in Thurso (a decision I always regretted!).

Although the design was excellent and unique, I always thought that some minor improvements were required, such as engine breathing and carburettor linkages. It was certainly not a wet weather car!

Friends who were Jowett owners at that time were Doug Rawson who lived in the Risley area and Per Guneratne of Milsom, Cumbria.

J. C. Douglas ... Egremont, Cumbria, February 1996

Doug is alive and well and is still a Javelin owner, living in Bradford. Per still lives in the same house in Milsom, and I, in fact, own one of the Javelins that he once owned: a PC model with a sunshine roof fitted registered FFR900.

A DECADE OF JOWETTS

My first Javelin, a 1949 model with a metal dash and registered FKY582, was bought from Claremont Garage in Bradford for £295 in 1954. Originally it was pale green with tan interior, but the doors had been filled with steel wool and newspaper and had been resprayed below the chrome strip with Morris Elfin Green. My first reaction on driving home was disappointment at the sluggish performance – having just traded in a Citröen Light 15 (1947). However, after attention to plugs and points and correcting ignition timing which was over 10 degrees out the performance improved considerably.

The first major problem occurred in the forecourt of York station when, on pulling away, a most horrendous knocking started. The engine still ran smoothly so I decided to try and get home – 3 miles. A taxi driver asked if it was a diesel! Immediately on arriving home I dropped the sump and found that the crankshaft had broken across the front web. Grabbing my wife's bike I rapidly pedalled to North Riding Motors, the local Jowett agents and bought a new crankshaft and set of bearing shells plus the bits of 'lead string' to go round timing case bolts and the felt seal for the back of the timing case (which always leaked anyway). The broken crankshaft was one of the 'machined' variety and was replaced with a 'black' one. During the two years that I ran this car covering about 50,000 miles the only real problem was blown head gaskets, which I used to replace at the roadside. I believe the problem was due to copper shims that set up the cylinder to give a proper 'nip' of the head gasket. If you got a watertight joint round the crankcase within a few hundred miles the head gasket would go. Setting the cylinders up enough with shims usually meant water leaks until the cylinder seals compressed enough to allow you to re-tighten the head bolts. The problem was overcome later by using rubber 'O' rings in grooves round the lower part of the cylinders and having a metal to metal contact between the cylinder flange and the crankcase. The same copper shims were used.

The only other irritation was water on the plugs. I tried the rubber disks without any success. The first puddle of water that you hit would reduce you to three or less cylinders. I had a plastic nozzle on my foot pump, which would blow the water out of the plug recess in the cylinder head. This nozzle was also vital to blow out the road grit and stones because on removing a plug a tiny pebble would drop down the plughole and lock the engine because at Top Dead Centre there is virtually no clearance between the piston crown and the lower side of the combustion chamber.

If you were brave enough you could try the starting handle and see if the stone would crush and hopefully get blown out through the exhaust, but usually it meant draining the coolant and slackening the head bolts, easing the joint and letting the offending foreign-body drop out. I have tried a blob of 'half dry' *Evostick* on a wire down the plughole and sometimes managed to fish out the stone.

Stan Pickard's first Javelin was a 1949 model with a metal dash and registered FKY582. It was bought from Claremont Garage in Bradford for £295 in 1954. Originally, it was pale green with tan interior, but the doors had been filled with steel wool and newspaper and had been resprayed below the chrome strip with Morris Elfin Green. His first reaction on driving the car home was disappointment at the sluggish performance – having just traded in a Citroën Light 15 (1947). However, after attention to plugs and points and correcting ignition timing, which was over 10 degrees out, the performance improved considerably. (Pickard)

Another shot of Stan's first Javelin registered FKY582. The car was purchased in Bradford for £295 in 1954 and sold in Bradford in 1956 for £210. (Pickard)

FKY582 again together with Stan's dog, which seems to get into most of his pictures! (Pickard)

The later type of 'lock in' plug caps was equally useless. Whilst they did give some protection from showers, heavier rain would get in between the cover plate and the head and would be more difficult to clear. The solution that I eventually adopted with total success was to use the original simple plug caps and fill the plug recess with Plasticene, moulding it round the cap. Later models which I had I converted to this system by removing the cover plates from the heads. The Plasticene did get a bit soft when the engine was hot but never caused any problems. It always came away with the plug cap leaving the plug recess clean and free from stones.

The steering on this car was always a bit heavy and one day during a parking manoeuvre there was an ominous crack, which on investigation disclosed a steering box broken in three places. Bootham Engineers of York welded the casting and re-machined it whilst I waited, at a total cost of £3 10s 6d. Incidentally I seem to recollect two different types of steering cross link. One was made from two channel pressings back to back with the end cone seals welded on whilst the other was an 'H' section forging but I can't remember which came first.

The brakes had a few idiosyncrasies being hydraulic at the front and mechanical at the rear with a 'floating' master cylinder. The two 'leading shoe' fronts would grab like mad if you set them up too close or didn't put enough chamfer on the leading edge after riveting on new linings.

The radiator fan forged rod supports used to break at regular intervals until more substantial ones were improvised. One other little source of annoyance – the rubber cups linking the carburettor intake tubes to the oil bath air cleaner in the bonnet always stuck to the bonnet when you lifted it and dropped off either onto the road or lodged up somewhere most awkward to reach. I have vivid recollections of trying to retrieve one whilst keeping my cuffs clean and putting my finger in the fan – fortunately without any permanent damage – but I felt very sick for a bit. I was sufficiently motivated to wire them on after that. I think later cars had a dry air cleaner instead of the oil bath.

In 1956 I traded this Javelin in at Moorside Motors, Bradford, for £210 against a 1951 Jupiter MK1 at £375. This car was registered HKU639 and started life as the 1951 Motor Show model and later as a demonstrator in London. It eventually went back to the works and I understand that at one time was used to develop the Series 111 engine. Anyway it was a car that gave me much pleasure and very little trouble. The car was white with red hood and trim but I believe had been gold originally. It had an oval-webbed shaft and whilst I have since learned that they also could break, at the time, it was very reassuring to know that it was the latest development.

I obtained Jowett's competition tuning notes and I got two spare heads from the breaker's yard so that I could work on them, without laying the car up. The combustion chambers were relieved and polished and the valve seats were machined out with high temperature inserts fitted. Competition valves were obtained (with I think stronger or double springs); inlet and exhaust ports were opened up and smoothed with much attention being given to the matching of ports, manifolds and carburettors. The exhaust pipe from the nearside head which joins the offside pipe after the manifold was lengthened to some incredibly complex formula which I have since forgotten and a new large bore exhaust system was fabricated.

I made a straight-through acoustic silencer by rolling some heavy but close wire mesh round two short pieces of tube and fixing with Jubilee clips. This mesh tube was then wrapped with coarse steel wool and bound with wire. This assembly was then put inside a steel tube (which I believe had been part of a conveyor) with the short pieces of tube sticking out at each end. The space between the steel wool wrapping and the case was stuffed with glass fibre (it was glass – not today's plastic stuff which burns) with end caps fitted and welded up. The result was a most melodic deep boom which completely transformed that irregular beat associated with the original manifolding.

Two journeys stick in my mind. The first a day at Silverstone for the British Grand Prix and the memory of driving home in the dark with the hood down, the powerful headlights carving a path through the night, the smells of the fields and trees, a responsive engine in perfect tune and that exciting exhaust echoing back from the walls and buildings.

The second one was an emergency business trip from York to Scarborough. During the night 4 inches of light snow had fallen but morning came crisp and brilliantly sunny. I had the hood down but the tonneau cover over the passenger seat. There was no-one else on the road and the memory of driving along the Malton Road at over 60 mph on virgin snow in the brilliant sunshine leaving a plume of powdered snow over 100 yards long behind me still seems as vivid as ever.

I was very sorry to part with the Jupiter but the impending arrival of a baby and the attendant problems of transporting pram, carry cot, bath and accessories between York, our home, and Bradford, our parents' home, almost weekly necessitated a change.

I sold the Jupiter to a garage in Clayton, Bradford, in 1958 for £325.

At this time petrol was on coupons due to the Suez Crisis (I think) and there were not many cars on the road other than those used for business. The garages were very short of work and North Riding Motors (the York Jowett agents) brought out a damaged Javelin which they had had in store for a couple of years to give their engineers something to do. This car, a 1951 model FVY900, was one that they sold new to an elderly couple. The car covered about 15,000 miles between 1951 and 1954 when it and the couple were involved in an accident. The car was not seriously damaged but the lady and gentleman were (no seat belts in those days!). The car was repaired by North Riding Motors and completely resprayed to showroom condition. It was put back into the couple's garage and not driven again for two years. North Riding Motors were then commissioned to renew tyres, brakes and anything else required. Exactly one mile from home on the first trip out the car was hit broadside on, so the old gentleman sold it to the garage for spares. North Riding Motors stored it for two more years (1958 now) and then decided to repair it. They took a truck across to Jowetts who I believe were at Howden Clough by then and collected all the necessary body, chassis and suspension parts required. They also borrowed the original chassis and body jigs.

Whilst I still had the Jupiter I had watched the progress of this rebuild with great interest. It was restored from the chassis upwards and painted and sealed at each stage. The body panels particularly round the scuttle and front wheel arches were continuously welded and not spotted as originally.

I used to look enviously at this car thinking that it would be way beyond my pocket when completed, but to cut a long story short knowing that I was looking for a Javelin I was offered it for £250 in primer, running but with all the trim and accessories filling the boot and back seat. Needless to say I grabbed it, hence the sale of the Jupiter.

The next job after fitting most of the interior trim and completing the wiring was the paint job. I decided to brush paint it as I had nowhere suitable for spray painting and it would have meant hiring equipment.

I racked my brains about the colour. I wanted something unique but tasteful and I tried to think of a colour which I had never seen on a car before. Then it struck me – lilac! Within six months of me using lilac, Peerless (a TR2 derivative) produced a slightly darker shade and then just twelve months later the millionth Morris Minor was produced in lilac. At least I headed the field.

Only a cursory rub down with wet and dry was required because every panel was either brand new in primer or immaculately original. I used Valspar because I had always liked it and they had a standard shade in lilac. The paint was bought in half-pint tins so that I could use a full tin at a session and have no problems with skinning. I used a new 2-inch brush with each tin after first washing it in soapy water and drying to remove any loose bristles. The paint was laid on fairly heavily and as I was working outside in hot sunshine it dried without running. It took about two weeks to paint – evenings and weekends, and if I remember correctly I used fifteen cans in all.

When it had finally hardened (about two weeks) I tried to rub it down with fine wet and dry but the paint tended to roll up. I tried Brasso and found this excellent. It was as though the friction melted the surface of the paint and it fused into a glass-like finish. Another advantage with Valspar is its unusual smell, it seemed to repel insects rather than attract them as some paints do.

The paint was bought at Dodgson's in York and they always used to keep me a parking place outside the shop so they could use my car as an advertisement for Valspar. Many garage-men asked who did the 'spray job'.

There was a sequel to this. One Saturday a lady called at my home doing a paint survey. After asking many questions about paint and which brands I knew she nearly fell over backwards when I showed her my Javelin painted with Valspar. She asked if I would test some paint on any current project – had I anything planned? I told her that I was going to paint the outside of the house and the outcome was that I had 2½ gallons of unnamed paint delivered free. It later turned out to be improved Valspar!

Anyway this Javelin was quite exceptional. The extra welding and precision assembly made the handling superb by stiffening the front section and suspension mountings. Corners used to be taken at speeds which have not been equalled by any car I have owned since. I drove this car fast and far but I did have a few mechanical troubles.

One of the first to manifest itself was the radiator fan blade. The car was fitted with a later type of fan; this had a centre spider to which the four blades were individually riveted. The opposing pairs were not at 90 degrees to each other. The fault was that the blade and spider broke through the rivet holes at 70 mph – the blade of course slicing through the radiator. Holt's Cataloy was quite new at the time so I pressed a wodge into the radiator core and this proved to be a permanent repair not affecting the operating temperature but losing the use of about three tubes I replaced the fan with the old type cut from a sheet with reinforced centre.

I was a member of York Motor Club and used the Javelin in all competitive events including rallies, hill climbs, driving tests and trials.

It was most at risk when being driven at constant high speed – 75-80 mph. Twice it broke pistons – the crown separating at the oil control ring. This was the weakest spot having drillings for two-thirds of the circumference and an expansion slot the rest of the way. Perhaps it was a partial seizure that caused it.

On another occasion it dropped a valve head at over 80 mph. The valve head was forged almost perfectly spherical between the piston and cylinder head until it knocked a hole through the piston crown. This was all between hearing the noise and getting the clutch down.

The trafficator 'carrots' were very vulnerable in York from cyclists moving up on the inside when you were signalling left at traffic lights. Once, when moving gently away from a start, second and third gear refused to engage. On dismantling the gearbox I found that a splined spacer had broken allowing the gears to float up and down the shaft. A new modified spacer was fitted and the trouble never re-occurred.

By this time I was getting quite slick at removing the engine, taking just over thirty minutes, which is close to Jowetts ' experts' time. Best replacement was 45 minutes to running.

I fitted a few modifications for competition work which included a navigator's hood, fitting from the fascia top and enclosing the glove locker. This had a map, light and allowed the navigator to read his maps and route charts without any reflections in the screen to distract the driver.

To make the handbrake 'fly off' I fitted a latch to hold the trigger release when pulled. On the roof I had a moveable rally light (now illegal), which I made from a Rover 12 gear change ball and socket, a Morris Minor steering rack gaiter, a carved wooden handgrip and a motorcycle horn button as a switch. The lamp was a Notek Blue Spot – a beautiful little spotlight and one of four no longer made. I had a headlamp flasher, twin driving lights and a spot reversing light. I also made a large armrest on the door that effectively wedged me between it and the central armrest.

One day, whilst cruising at about 45 mph (unusual for me), a heavy vibration started, accompanied by a peculiar feel about the steering. Upon investigation I found that the offside front wheel had split and the flange opened up for about a third of the circumference. I seem to remember that those Dunlop rims were always bleeding round the rivets joining the centre to the rim and I was constantly tightening up the rivets with a hammer and block.

On one of the numerous occasions when I was removing the engine and struggling with the prop shaft bolts, I felt the car move above me. Hastily shooting a glance at the pillar jack I realised that it was leaning sideways by about 30 degrees and rapidly moving further. I don't remember getting out from beneath the car but I was in time to see the jack finally tear the jacking socket away from the chassis and the car flopping down on the hubs. I was too concerned with checking for damage to think about my escape until later.

Many rallies, driving tests and motor sport events were entered in this car and whilst not often figuring in the awards we never really disgraced ourselves; after all, we were competing with MGAs, TR2s, stripped Anglias, and garage-sponsored entries.

One dark and very wet night we were about halfway into the Club's premier rally and doing extremely well when during a speed test on Full-Sutton Airfield the throttle cable broke. Fortunately it was at the accelerator end and by letting a bit of slack out from the carburettor end I was able to reconnect it and we were away again. Determined to regain the advantage that we once held we pressed on along the narrow country lanes around York. Timed events were permitted on public roads in those days. Near Bugthorpe, of all places, we attacked a humpbacked bridge. As soon as my headlights came down again and I could see the road, I thought good straight ahead, and dropped my lead boot on the throttle. Almost instantly, through the rain I saw straight ahead was not the road but a farm track barred by a very substantial looking gate and the road in fact bore sharply to the left between high walls and hedges. I managed to correct my error but halfway round this sharp bend I realised that the farmer had been leading beet (a local crop) and the road was covered in wet clay from the tractor wheels. By this time things were starting to happen that I had very little control over until a gap in the wall appeared and I managed to tweak the car through. I can remember mixed feelings of relief and triumph but just as I was beginning to congratulate myself we fell off the end of the world – the field was ten feet down!

Not one of the three of us in the car really remembers turning over and the impact, or the few seconds after but as soon as we found that we were all more or less unhurt we tried to get out. All four doors were jammed solid; the car was upside down with the bonnet and windscreen embedded in the mud. There was a smell of burning oil, a frighteningly strong smell of petrol and we were aware of being soaked with fluid dripping on to us. We didn't exactly panic but getting out featured quite high on our list of priorities. Syd, showing commendable motivation, managed to kick out a side window and we all extruded at high speed. It was then that we realised that it was battery acid dripping on to us from the two 6 volts under the back seat and we became aware of the burning on our heads, faces and hands. Great clumps of wet grass were used to wash ourselves down and the following day all our clothes fell to bits.

Turning our attention to the car we realised that the ignition and lights were still on. The real shock was in seeing how much rubbish we had in the car. When it is all piled up together in the roof it is quite staggering.

Thoughts of getting home now started to worry us. At 2 a.m. on a very wet Sunday morning out in the country there was little chance of anyone passing by. We were at the tail of the field after our throttle cable episode and the rally marshals would take a main road direct route so we were on our own.

We managed to swivel the car round on its roof and then tried to roll it onto its wheels. It looks so easy nowadays with modern rally cars but the Javelin weighing over a ton in sticky mud was different. Twice we got it up on two wheels and twice we had to let it drop back. Eventually we got it back onto its roof and with a concerted effort, in a continuous movement, rolled it right over onto its wheels. I think that the poor thing suffered more damage in recovery than in the original impact. After driving through about three fields we eventually got back onto the road and drove home with no windscreen, the roof about a foot lower than normal and the rain still bucketing down.

I had a long battle with my insurance company who said the car was a write-off and offered me £250. The insurance assessor who came from Middlesboro set the value but I had three offers also from Middlesboro by phone of £275. I couldn't help feeling there was a racket operating. Eventually I settled for £300 in lieu of repairs and I rebuilt the car myself. I sold the engine for £50 and the body shell for £150.

My next car, a 1952 De Luxe Javelin LWT688 in immaculate bottle green, I bought for £395 in York. This car was the ultimate Javelin, which represented Jowett's peak of achievement. It had a full instrument panel, as of course had the previous 1951 model, but whereas this had its instruments set behind a wooden panel with chamfered cut-outs, this one had flush fitted instruments with chrome bezels. This car proved to be the most refined but sadly my last Jowett. I drove it in a slightly more restrained manner and revelled in its luxury for over two years.

During my ten years of exclusive Jowett ownership I purchased three other Javelins on behalf of friends and assisted them with their maintenance.

The local Jowett agents, North Riding Motors, often contacted me for spares and I had a tour of Jowetts when they moved to Howden Clough and saw the rows of Series 3 engines being run on test beds. Incidentally they gave me a Jowett Emblem Tie Pin, which I was very proud of but I'm afraid it has since been lost.

Stan's second Javelin was a 1951 model registered FVY900 pictured on a snowy day near Pickering in January 1961. (Pickard)

Another snowy day with Stan's second Javelin FVY900, this time on the North Yorkshire Moors in February 1960. (Pickard)

FVY900 after its crash on a rally near Bubwith, York, in October 1961. It is parked at the Jowett agents in York, North Riding Motors, awaiting the Insurance Assessors. (Pickard)

This was Stan's last Javelin: a 1952 example registered LWT688. It was bought in 1961 for £395 and sold in 1963 for £285. (Pickard)

A very grainy photo of Stan's 1951 Jupiter registered HKU639; the car was originally a 1951
Motor Show exhibit and later a demonstrator car at the London Showrooms. It later returned
to Idle and was used as a test bed for the Series 3 engine. Stan bought the car for £425 in
1956 but sold it in 1958 for £325 due to children coming along, and a saloon being necessary
to carry prams, etc. (Pickard)

In 1976 I saw my old Jupiter HKU639 at a garage in Bingley looking very sad
and neglected, now painted red, and strangely five years later an acquaintance told
me a friend of his was restoring a Jupiter in Leicester. I told him about mine and
asked him to check the registration number. He later told me that it was HKU639,
but unfortunately I have lost contact with him and don't even know his name.

This is the story of my happy recollections of ten years of Jowett ownership and
I hope that it might be of interest to other enthusiasts and perhaps trigger some
almost forgotten memories. One day perhaps I might own another ...

Stan Pickard ... Bradford, West Yorkshire, June 1987

*HKU639 was chassis number E1/SA/339; it was the Earls Court show car and
was later used as a demonstrator car at the London Showrooms before returning
to Jowett Cars Ltd to be used as a test-bed for the Series 3 engine. The car has
in fact survived and is being restored at the present time.*

MEMORIES OF JUPITER OWNERS

JUPITER REGISTERED BCW140

I owned a 1951 Jowett Jupiter between 1967 and 1969; its registration number was BCW140. This car had been purchased by a friend of mine at the Preston Motor Auctions in 1964, where he paid £40 for it. I obtained it from him in a straight swop for my split-screen Beetle, and I certainly got the worst of the deal!

When I got the car it had no dynamo or charging circuit, no hood and a rotten interior, with rotten floorboards etc. It did, however, pass an MOT test and I used the car as everyday transport. It was fitted with a Javelin engine with the usual badly worn crankshaft but, as happens with unusual cars, I was told of a man in Preston who was breaking a complete Jupiter.

So I bought from him a Jupiter engine, which was in good condition, seat and other essentials and ended up with a fairly smart car, although it was never reliable.

I should add that at my time of ownership, I had very little spare cash and had to keep the car on the road on a veritable shoestring. Fortunately, at that time there were plenty of scrap yards and farm yards with rusted-out Javelins in them. This gave me a good source of cheap parts, many of which were given to me.

In 1969 I went to work in Plymouth, but as I could not trust the car to make the arduous 350-mile journey, I sold it to a Blackpool car dealer. I do not remember his name, but I do remember I was delighted with the £40 he gave me for it. So after this I enjoyed my weekends without getting covered in oil.

I never saw the car again.

David Huntington ... St Annes, Lancashire, February 1996

This car was chassis number E1/SA/463; it was originally supplied to the Jowett agents Hebden Brothers Ltd, Burnley, on 19 November 1951 and was originally green with beige leather trim. The first owner of the car was Mr J. C. Pollard of 367 Padiham Road, Burnley, who first registered it for the road on 26 November 1951. Sadly, the car is not on the list of known survivors.

Class winner at Le Mar

JOWETT JUPITER

The Jupiter Mark IA

years running

JUPITER REGISTERED FVG87

In 1954 I bought a late Mark 1 Jupiter from the Jowett agents Clarke's of Pirbright; it was registered FVG87 and was coloured red with beige trim. I think the car was first registered in Norwich.

At the end of the same year I part exchanged it for a new Triumph TR2 at College Motors, Bristol. I think it was then bought by a Somerset farmer.

In 1957, during or just after the Suez Crisis petrol-rationing period, I met a technical representative from the instrument manufacturers, George Kent, whose father owned a Jupiter. The rep looked up the registration number on some of his father's petrol coupons and found it was my old car FVG87!

I will give you details of my experiences of the car: it was a unique car with a charm all of its own. For sheer joy of motoring, and before we had any motorways (and hardly any dual carriageways), I once drove the car almost non-stop for eighteen hours, covering some 720 miles. The running average speed was, I remember, exactly 40 miles per hour and the fuel consumption was, I believe, fractionally under 30 miles per gallon.

Somewhere buried in my archives I have the tabulated record of this day, but not the precise route, although I know it was something like this, Bristol – Stow-on-the-Wold – Warwick – Oxford – Winchester – Exeter – Land's End – Exeter – Salisbury – Bristol.

The chassis and bodywork were superb, the controls were feather light and I used to change gear with just one finger. As regards handling, I found that the rear end broke away too easily, but correction and control was never a problem. If I had owned the car in later years I would have tried the trick of fitting radials to the rear with cross-plys to the front. Generally the 'ride' was excellent.

Mechanically the car was a near disaster – not long after I purchased the car the pistons and liners were drawn to reveal 'pick-up' on one piston, almost certainly due to the first owner not running it in properly. Clarke's supplied new pistons and liners without so much as a murmur and the engine was rebuilt and I carefully ran it in. Later I experienced failure of the clutch plate centre spider (the only clutch failure I have ever experienced) and in the September a hairline crack appeared in one of the cylinder heads, so with much reluctance it had to go.

The one maddening thing about the car was a flat spot at 2,000 rpm; it was just like switching the ignition off. The trick was to push through 2,000 rpm as smartly as possible (I am sure a carburettor specialist could have tuned this out, but I learnt to live with it).

There was also a brief propshaft vibration at just on 68 mph (4,000 rpm); here again + or – 2 mph and it went. The snag was that 68 mph was a nice cruising speed.

An acquaintance who had a Jupiter kept a spare engine in the garage! – Jowett folks with whom I corresponded with briefly only claimed 4,000 miles before a major engine overhaul, which was not good at all even in 1954.

But it was a car one never forgets – a sheer delight to own and drive despite its shortcomings. And I seem to remember that one could raise and lower the excellent hood without having to leave the driver's seat.

I hope that these ramblings are of some interest to you. [*You bet!* ... *NS*]

John Armstrong ... Milinthorpe, Cumbria, February 1996

FVG87 was chassis number E3/SA/903 and was dispatched to the Jowett agents Reliance Garage of Norwich on 27 April 1953. It was originally red with beige leather trim. I am pleased to say that the car is a survivor and is in excellent roadworthy condition.

JUPITER SGX64

I had a letter published in the Western Gazette on 6 December 1991, which led to some great correspondence with John Doran over a four-year period. I will start with his original letter and take it from there!

I had a Jupiter way back in 1952 when I was living in Ghana, West Africa, its WAC registration number out there was AD1233. I drove this car all over that part of the world for the three years I was out there. Finally, when I returned to the UK, I drove it back home, with a bit of help from the French Army – it was an ideal car for the dirt roads out there.

I then had the car overhauled by Jowetts in Idle prior to my next posting to Germany, where I stayed for the next year. Whilst out there I became a member of the Army's four-car rally team known as The White Horse Motor Club, Hanover.

Finally I sold the car in 1963 for £75 to a Rootes Group garage in London, as I no longer had anywhere to keep it. They were going to drive it off to the local scrap yard to be scrapped – what a pity; I bet it would have been worth a 'bomb' now!

John Doran ... Gillingham, Dorset, January 1991

Needless to say, I was delighted with this letter, so I rang John and later wrote to him to tell him that his car had not been scrapped and had been restored to a very high standard by the late Ben Shaw (a Jowett Car Club stalwart). Needless to say, he was delighted with this news and was going to arrange going to see the car again. His next letter follows:

Again, very many thanks for your letter and enclosure. I have now found seventeen photos (all rather small) of the car when it was out in West Africa. I have also found my article, 'A Journey through Africa', which is too long.

Perhaps I could give you an article stating at the end when Rootes in London drove the car away to the scrap heap and reading your article in the *Western Gazette* – contacting you, to be told the terrific news of the 'resurrection' of the car. Then the story of the car in West Africa from 1952 (registered AD1233) – Then the trip from Accra to the River Niger and west to Dakar with assistance from the French Army, back to France and then England. The big overhaul at Jowett's in Idle and my rallying in Hanover, Germany, (then registered K250BZ) then back to the UK where it was registered SGX64, and to what I thought was the end in September 1963. If Ben Shaw was still alive he would have been interested in the car's previous life. I cannot help feeling that he must have found some African red dust in some corner! Of course in Germany the car had snow and ice in the Harz Mountains to contend with, so there was quite a change for 'Jupi' after Africa!

In March 1991, John wrote again to say that he had now reduced down the length of his 'A Journey through West Africa' article down to a more manageable three pages (I would have been happy with the original longer version). He also sent a copy to Pete Dixon, who owned the car at that time. The article was featured in By Jupiter *issue 2, 1991 – the club magazine for the Jupiter Owner's Auto Club. I will publish it here as well, as I was delighted to receive this article from John at the time.*

JOWETT JUPITER SGX64

It was in September 1963 when my Jowett Jupiter SGX64 was traded in for a new Hillman Minx costing £775. The Rootes Group in London allowed me £75 for the Jupiter. After that, my only comfort was that I had two extra days a week free instead of maintaining that car.

It was at the end of 1990 that I noticed a picture of Noel Stokoe with his Javelin in the North Dorset edition of the *Western Gazette* wanting to know if any readers were past owners of Jowett cars. I wrote to him saying that I owned a Jowett Jupiter in 1952 in the Gold Coast, West Africa. Having established the registration number, I had the surprise of my life when he told me that the car was still in existence, as I thought it must have been scrapped in 1963. But there it was in the Jowett Car Club National Weekend Official Programme, which Noel sent me, with Ben Shaw at the wheel. He could not have known the history of this car when it started life in West Africa on WAC plates, registered AD1233.

I bought the car in 1952 from a Syrian-owned garage called Berberi Mallickin, Accra, Ghana, then called the Gold Coast. I was in the Army in the RWAFF so the car went where army trucks went, and those roads were mostly corrugated dust tracks.

Before I was due to return to England, I wrote to Jowett Cars Ltd about driving back and asked them for a list of spare parts that I might need. They told me that in the 1920s two two-seater models crossed the Sahara from West to East and after the war a Bradford Utility crossed the Sahara from North to South. So I said I would cross it from South to North.

This would mean travelling north to Upper Volta, then to Wagadugu and continue to the River Niger to Bourem near Timbuctu in Mali where one would pick up the main route across the Sahara through Algeria to the Mediterranean. However permission to go this way was turned down and out of the question.

We used to have manoeuvres with the French Army who were based along the Southern Sahara and by chance there was a visiting group of officers from Dakar staying with us in Accra. They suggested a route taking in their bases, which with their maps and conditions plus Military permission, made things much easier. So that is exactly what we did.

It was now April 1955 when we started the journey north for Wagadugu in the Upper Volta, where my batman came from, so he had a free trip home. Unfortunately I could not cross the frontier near Lawra in the North West corner of the Gold Coast because of flooding of the Black Volta. This meant we had to travel an extra 150 miles in the wrong direction.

There was a shorter route which meant persuading some villagers to carry the car across the high banks of a small river. They did this with great excitement; we were then able to get to a place called Leo. Having crossed the frontier there was a very straight track that must have been one hundred miles long, with no other vehicles about. I decided to drive all night in the cool, hoping to reach the larger road by dawn. It was on this stretch that trouble came when one of the front wheels broke loose from its ball and socket joint, rendering the car un-steerable. My batman was not keen to get out of the car, as all around there were reflections of eyes in the headlights, but we were unable to make out what was out there in the dark.

I made repairs using wire to bind the joints together, which seemed to work but something had to be done soon before coping with the main road which had very large corrugations and pot holes in it. Huge Trans-Sahara lorries with two engines used these roads and the Jupiter would have to travel at a minimum speed of 60 miles an hour, so as to skim the tops of the corrugations otherwise the car would have been shaken to pieces.

We were lucky to find what must have been the only house in the area occupied by a very pleasant French Canadian Missionary and his wife. At the back of the house they had a huge workshop where he was able to make the spare parts required. His repair work lasted until I reached England.

After two days with the Missionary, I deposited my batman near Wagadugu, so I was then on my own driving west for Bobo Diulasso; this was the first French Army Base on the trip.

I stayed there for a few days while the car was serviced and the dust cleaned out of it, even the dynamo was taken to pieces. One could never drive with the hood up, as the dust would still get in and swirl around inside the car, which made it impossible to see out.

The next base was Bamako on the Niger River; the temperature was 110 degrees Fahrenheit and the two jerry cans of water behind the seat were very hot, there was no need to boil the water for coffee. The film in the camera frizzled in the heat, so many pictures taken on the trip were lost. Between Bamako and Dakar the first stretch of road was impassable, so the car went by Goods Train for a quarter of the way and I followed the train by air.

Arriving at Dakar, I once again met up with the same army officers to whom I had talked in Accra. I spent five days there before embarking on the SS *Djeune* with the car. I stayed for a day in the Canary Islands before calling in at Tangier. I should have disembarked here for Gibraltar but went on to Marseilles. I had no official papers for Europe, so the only way out was to join the RAC and collect the papers from them in Paris. By now the car was burning oil, but at least I had not yet had a puncture. A good advert for 'Goodyear Super Export' tyres!

I drove to Paris from Marseilles and collected the paperwork before making my way to the ferry and to England. I arranged to take the car back to the Jowett factory in Idle, Bradford, where they gave the car a complete overhaul which included the fitting of a reconditioned engine. Unfortunately this replacement engine did not have the covers over the plugs which the original had, so after that I was always in trouble with water and stones getting into the plug wells.

I was now stationed in Germany, and so had a year there where I started rallying with the 'White Horse Club' of Hanover. I was stationed in Goslar in the Harz Mountains, so the Jupiter now had to put up with ice and snow. It had to be reregistered in Germany and its new number became K250BZ. I was stationed here between 1955 and 1956 and it kept this number throughout.

This Jupiter has had a particularly interesting life, having been owned by John Doran in 1952 whilst he was working in Ghana, West Africa. At that time, it was registered AD1233. He and the car spent three years out there. At the end of this time, with a bit of help from the French Army, he drove it to England, crossing the Sahara Desert! This picture was taken on the grass plains of Accra. (Doran)

The Jupiter being loaded onto a train at Bamoto. (Doran)

This is another picture of John Doran on a hot day in Ghana. After his posting in Germany, he returned to the UK bringing the Jupiter with him. It was re-registered in the UK SGX64. John finally parted with the car for £75 and was under the impression that it had been scrapped in the early 1960s. I was able to tell him that the car was still alive and well and since then a reunion has since taken place with the present owner of the car. (Doran)

Final shot of John Doran's Jupiter in its West African guise registered AD1233, later to be re-registered SGX64 in the UK. (Doran)

I kept my old Africa Coast International plate as a memento. In Goslar I found a hood maker who fitted a very thick nylon hood to the car, which was now essential in the cold and snow.

I was in a four-car Army Rally Team in events with the Allgemeinen Deutschen Automobil Club and travelled all over Germany with them in various rallies and competitions. In December 1955 HQ at Northag held a 'Crossed Swords' Rally over a distance of 400 miles taking in the forest roads. We came in second to an Aston Martin, who won by just two points.

It was April 1956 when I returned with the car to England and settled down to a much calmer life; this was when the car was allocated its third registration number SGX64. As detailed above, I kept the car until 1963, which is when I thought it had been scrapped.

As mentioned above, the car was restored from a very poor condition to concours standard by the late Ben Shaw – a stalwart of the Jowett Car Club. The car's first outing was the JCC Rally in Cheltenham in 1975. At the time of this correspondence (1991), the car was owned by Pete Dixon. By 1993, he had sold it to John Blazé. I passed his details on to John Doran. This led to this lovely letter from John.

At long last the old car with John Blazé turned up here for us to see after so many years (1963). I had no idea that Peter Dixon had sold it to John. At least we are on route for him to call in from his home in Cornwall to his work in London. I was able to find the old badges from the Jupiter and the West Africa Coast number plate and also the badge of the regiment from when I was in Germany. I gave these to him and he was pleased to have them passed on.

Thank you again to you for placing your article in our local paper that has started all of this!

He is a nice fellow with a good sense of humour, which I think you need to have, also he is very interesting. We took photos of course for the records.

Many thanks again for putting us all in touch – it has been very exciting.

John Doran ... Gillingham, Dorset, May 1995

I have to say I have great pleasure in tracking down ex-Jowett owners, and to have a series of letters like this gives me great satisfaction, as this information would have been lost had I not placed an add in his local paper, which I have done with at least 100 other local papers and magazines over the last twenty-five years.

JUPITER REGISTERED BHG427

I raced and rallied a Mark 1 Jupiter in 1953 and 1954. I sold the car to a young lady from Haigh near Wigan, and from time to time since then I have tried to find it, should it still exist. Sadly I have no chassis number for the car, but I can confirm that the registration number was BHG427. The number seemed to cause some doubt in the Jupiter Owners' Auto Club, but as you can see from the enclosed copy letters that I was able to confirm that the number is correct.

If, as a result of greater interest now in Classic Cars you now have any further record of my car, I would be most interested to hear from you. If the car does still exist, I would be most anxious to try and buy it back.

Does the Jupiter Owners' Auto Club still exist? [*Yes, it is alive and well ... NS*]

Tom Blackburn ... Longridge, Preston, February 1996

The copy letter he sent with this letter, which was addressed to JOAC in May 1983, is interesting, as he gave details of the car while it was in his ownership.

Thank you for your letter. I have picked up my photo album and can confirm that the car's registration number was BHG427, as it is clearly visible on several pictures. But I regret that I do not have a copy of its log book, as photocopiers were not in existence in 1953.

I bought the car in the spring of 1953, and I think it was one of a large batch that were probably built in 1952 and remained unsold for a while. It was purchased through A. E. Rimmer Ltd of Chorley, near Preston, who at the time were Insurance Brokers and on the edge of the Motor Trade. Mr Albert Rimmer, the proprietor, is still alive and I see him occasionally, but I think it will be doubtful if he has records going that far back. I can confirm that the original colour of the car was British Racing Green.

I have a copy of the book by Edmund Nankivell, and the references in the book to Mr Blackburn do in fact refer to me. I well remember too the 1953 Six-Hour Relay Race, but owing to mechanical problems in the rest of the team I seem to recall doing just over 3½ hours out of the total of 6. It was a very wet day indeed, and my fiancée, who is now my wife, came with me. She remembers me collecting her in Preston at 3.30 in the morning; she was made even wetter as there was only an aero screen for protection while we drove to Silverstone. I then went off in the car for practising, did the race then drove home again with her that evening. Unfortunately I cannot remember where we finished in this particular race, but I do have somewhere in my attic all the programmes for the events in which I competed.

Regarding that particular event, I enclose a copy of a photograph which shows me just about to pass Baker's Land Rover, and I clearly remember how well it went and how brave the driver was. The other copies show the car running as a saloon, which is again referred to in the book in the Bolton-le-Willows driving tests in March 1954. Another in the Lancashire Automobile Club Morecambe Rally in May 1954. Unfortunately, the not uncommon problem of a broken crankshaft ended this event during the night section.

I drove the car in several other events and enclose again a couple of photocopies taken at the USAF Trophy Race Meeting at Snetterton in July 1953. That unfortunately was the meeting when Bobby Baird was killed in his Ferrari when he slid off the track, the car rolled over and the gear lever punctured a lung. Other events which I remember were the Bo'ness Hill Climb when Ted Lund and I shared my car; that was in September 1953; in August 1953 I was at a race meeting at Charter Hall. We ran the car in the Highland Three-Day Rally at Easter 1954, but I can't remember where we finished other than having a plaque somewhere in a box for a first class award. The event which I remember best was the Jeans Gold Cup Rally which took place in heavy snow in the spring of 1954, when TR2s were just coming onto the scene. My brother reminded me of that event this morning because he was navigating for me, we were determined to beat the TRs whatever happened, and ten miles from the end of the rally we absolutely had it in the bag. Unfortunately we stopped to push some people out of the snow on Buttertubs Pass and we were unable to get going ourselves afterwards. Instead of a glorious win we had a 'Did not Finish'.

If this information would be of any more use to you, I think I could find some of the results from the records I have somewhere at home. Both my brother and I remember the car with great affection and if it does still exist, and providing the price was not too ridiculous, I would be possibly interested in buying it back for restoration.

Tom Blackburn ... May 1983

Sadly, some twenty-five years on from this correspondence, the car has never turned up, so I am sure it must have been scrapped. This is a shame, as three other BHGs have survived – 181, 633 and 703 – but no sign of 427.

SPECIAL-BODIED JUPITER REGISTERED MGP999

I take *Classic & Sportscar* and had already read the piece about the Jowett Jupiter Harold Radford special, which caused me a great deal of sadness. Many years ago I had a letter from a man living in Scotland, asking me to confirm whether I had ever owned the Jupiter he claimed to have, so I wrote and told him a little of its history whilst in my hands. I presume, without a record of our correspondence, that this would be the same George Mitchell to whom you refer to in your letter.

I now enclose three photos of the car, registration number MGP999, which I owned from late 1951, when I took delivery of it from Harold Radford, until I sold it in 1954 or 1955, by which time Jowett had gone out of business. The first is a 'showroom' picture which had been taken by Radfords. The other two are of me racing the car in the Six-Hour Relay race at Silverstone in 1952. I must insist that you return these to me, as they are the only photos I have of the car, and are of great personal interest and value to me.

The specification was a conventional two-seater on the standard Jupiter chassis, but had an easily detachable windscreen, which could be replaced by a fold-flat racing screen on the driver's side. It had virtually no boot, but reasonable stowage space behind the seats even when the hood was dismantled. Radford wanted to hang bumpers and chrome grills, etc. but I dissuaded him, having just what my friends used to call a 'chicken wire' grill in each of the three apertures – easy to clean and remove, and a good deal lighter than the nonsense they had sketched. For racing the scrutineers made me remove the spats from the rear wheels and also the centre grille, on the grounds that these were insecure and could fly off under impact!

It is true that I took the car on honeymoon – it was an ideal tourer in the sun. It had a great capacity for consuming throttle cables – I was on my third by the time we got to some remote corner of the Dolomites, where it expired again. Wedging the throttle open and driving on the ignition key I made my way precariously to the nearest village, where I was directed to what I can only describe as a local blacksmith. Yes – by the signs he was a dab hand at repairing graunched bicycles, prams, even small tractors. Without a common language I explained my problem and retreated to the nearest café. Two hours later he proudly showed me that the car worked, he demanded about 10s and off I went. I never had any more trouble with the throttle cable to the day I sold the car!

I have been tempted to write to Mr Mitchell to see if he would like to sell the car – but have not done so, mainly because although I have the space to store the car, I have neither the time, or the means to restore it. I would certainly be interested to hear the fate of it, if it falls into one of your club member's hands. I believe I could even search out a pair of head gaskets and some bearings for the crankshaft that I had as continental spares, although I make no promises.

It was my great regret that, during Motor 100 at Silverstone last year, I did not have time to contact a representative of the Jowett Car Club. Being host to such a vast gathering, I had to spend so much time with VIPs and our own team of organisers, and really only had time to spare with the Aston Martin people, to whom I had lent my own vintage car, one of the ex-team DB2s.

The Hon. Gerald Lascelles ... Rendcomb, Cirencester, May 1986

This special-bodied Jupiter was built by Harold Radford for Gerald Lascelles, the Queen's cousin, and registered MGP999. He took delivery of the car in 1951 and ran it until late 1954 or early 1955. He used the car to go on honeymoon in, but broke several throttle cables whilst on the trip. He also drove it in the 1952 Six-Hour Relay Race at Silverstone. He is seen here in the car. (Lascelles)

In the above letter from Gerald Lascelles, he made reference to the 'Motor 100', which was a huge event. I joined the Jowett Car Club in August 1984 and bought my first Jowett, a 1952 Jupiter registered JBE4, in February 1985 (which I still have) and attended Motor 100 at Silverstone with my wife, Jane, and my young son, Ben. This was the wettest weekend I can ever remember; it should have been a great weekend, as just about every car club in the country was represented there, but I have to say, it was not a lot of fun, as we were soaked to the skin over the whole weekend!

To bring things right up to date regarding the Gerald Lascelles car, during last year there had been several references to special-bodied Jupiters in the Classic & Sportscar *magazine. The June issue carried a letter from Richard Palmer saying that his father, Tony, had bought two special-bodied Jupiters in 1989 from the well-known Jowett collector George Mitchell of Sheriffmuir, near Dunblane, Scotland, where they had spent many years in a field. Both cars were in a derelict state, but Tony brought them back to his home in Yorkshire and got on with restoring them. Sadly, Tony died suddenly when he was only part-way through restoring the Radford-bodied Jupiter.*

The magazine also printed three very small photos of the car, one when new, one of the car languishing in the Scottish field and one of the car as it is now in its part-restored state. The article confirmed that the other special-bodied (an Armstrong) had already been sold. It also stated that Tony had removed the body and restored the chassis and engine of the Radford-bodied car, but it had then been in storage since his death. The body had been refitted, so the car

Harold Radford built two special-bodied Jupiters, both to very different designs. This car was the one owned by Gerald Lascelles and is now under restoration after languishing in a Scottish field since the mid-1960s. It will create a great deal of interest when it is finally back on the road after such a long time. The second car built by Harold Radford was registered WAR182 and was in attendance at the Centenary Rally in Wakefield; a picture of it is featured in the colour section.

was looking like something almost complete, but I understand that the electrics, interior and paintwork still have to be done.

The article finished off by saying that the car might now be for sale; in view of this, I contacted Richard, who confirmed that this was the case. I therefore placed an advert on his behalf in the Jowett Car Club magazine, The Jowetteer, and the Jupiter Owners Auto Club magazine, By Jupiter! to see if a buyer could be found.

I am pleased to say that it was bought by a well-known Jowett collector, so the car is now safe and will finally be restored – it is said that the last time that the car was taxed and registered for the road was in 1957, so it certainly has been a long wait!

JUPITER REGISTERED BHG703

I read with interest your plea in *The Daily Telegraph*, and confess to owning several Javelins and my pride and joy a Jowett Jupiter, which was a 1952 example coloured ivory and registered BHG703. This car was purchased from the Jowett agents Buntings of Harrow in 1965 for £80.

I sold it in 1968 or 1969 to Ben Shaw of Chorleywood. Ben was Engineer in Charge of Services at Wembley Outside Broadcast Base of the BBC Outside Broadcast Team. Needless to say the mechanical workshop he had was well adapted for Jowett repairs. I had my brake drums skimmed and various minor repairs done there! I worked then as a Television Cameraman at Wembley and used the car to various outside broadcasts around the country.

Ben died a few years ago and I have no idea what happened to his collection of Jowetts including my Jupiter. During my ownership it took me and a friend and all our camping and climbing equipment all over this country. We also took it to the Swiss Alps on a climbing holiday and attracted admiring glances right through France!

The car never let me down on the road, but on one occasion an intermittent fuel pump was coaxed back to life at West Wittering with a nail file between the points and some gentle tapping with a road-side stone! The little ball joint on the top of the gear change snapped cleanly off on my last gear change before parking her in the garage!

The electrics were prone to a disconcerting habit of fusing all the lights when travelling at speed; this was finally traced to a perished grommet and a rubbing wire on the feed to the number plate light. The HT side of the ignition was prone to water ingress until I fitted aircraft-type connectors. But apart from these events above, the car was very reliable. I never had so much fun with a car, or lost so little money on it – £30 in three years.

I occasionally come across the North Yorkshire Moors in my boring Vauxhall, and I did see a green Jupiter last year on the Scarborough to Whitby road – perhaps it was you! [*I would guess it was, as at the time I was the only Jupiter owner in the area. There are two now, but the other one is ivory ... NS*]

Apologies for the handwriting, but I would be interested to hear from you if BHG703 was still alive. [*Yes it is, as detailed in the note above about BHG427 ... NS*]

Alex Thomas ... Berkhampsted, Herts, March 1996

JUPITER REGISTERED PTT243

As requested, I have written down for you my memories of Jowett cars, following your request that was published in the *Auto Express* magazine.

I have had a somewhat varied career beginning at the age of eighteen after first attending a motor engineering college while waiting for call-up for National

Service (which never materialised as I failed the medical) and it was during this time that I had my first encounter with Jowett cars and vans.

There were a few Bradford vans belonging to customers of this garage, Bertram Cowen's of Streatham, South West London, with which I was involved but I have to admit to you that I was not very interested in these. However, Cowens were agents for Jowetts, so when they got in their first Javelin, I have to say I was enthralled.

The first time I ever drove a Javelin was when I was about twenty years old and was asked to go with a customer in his brand new one and bring it back to the garage. To my horror the drive back entailed coming through the West End of London via Hyde Park Corner during the mid-morning rush in what was in those days heavy traffic, and I was scared stiff of damaging it, but I managed to get back in one piece, I have to say that I fell in love with the car immediately.

This must have been late 1949 or early 1950, when I had been driving for just over a year. After this my heart had been stolen by the Javelin, and being so keen, I was able to work on them quite a lot, and from what I remember, a large amount of this concerned problems with the gearboxes.

When the Jupiter came on the scene I wanted one! Unfortunately, due to my low wages there was no chance that I would be able to afford to buy one. It must have been in about 1956 that, having been bequeathed some money by an elderly relative, I was able to start thinking about it.

I eventually came across a second-hand one in a garage in Croydon and fell for it immediately. Although it was in poor condition there did not appear to be anything wrong that I could not handle, and I bought it for £400. It had been advertised as 'first registered in 1953' and being of a far too trusting nature I took it to mean that it was new in 1953. It turned out to be a 1951 model which was first registered abroad, I believe in Nigeria. [*Yes, the Jowett factory records show that the car was chassis number E1/SA/229 and had been shipped to a Mrs D. Yull of Accra on 19 September 1951. It was originally in British Racing Green with beige leather trim ... NS*] It also turned out that at some time it had had a front-end shunt which had put severe strain on the steering column and gear-change (but more of this later).

Anyway I took it home and started having fun with it, until within a very short time it became apparent that it had serious gearbox trouble. So I took it back to the showroom expecting to have it repaired but no – 'I'm sorry sir there is no guarantee.' Back home my father was furious and was straight on the phone threatening solicitors attention, but still they would not budge. Since by this time I had a pretty good knowledge of them, I tried to cool the situation down by suggesting that I would do the necessary work myself if they supplied the new parts as necessary. This they eventually agreed to, so all was well again.

The main problem was oil consumption – I swear it used more than petrol! I therefore had the engine out, checked it all over and found everything to be acceptable, even if not in perfect condition, so I fitted a set of Duaflex rings and tried again – I don't think it ever used any more oil.

I later had a new vinyl hood made for it in a shade of green slightly lighter than the British Racing Green body and a three-piece wrap-round rear window, and it looked beautiful. I now had my dreamed-of Jupiter registered PTT243 and I set out to have some enjoyment.

The first great adventure was to visit the British Grand Prix at Aintree in 1957 with my old friend Ted Billison who I had known from school days in 1941. In the early sixties we became related when we married two sisters and after sixty-plus years we still spend time together. We set out to drive to Aintree overnight intending to call on a friend who lived near Stoke on Trent and have a rest and breakfast there before carrying on to Aintree.

I did of course manage to flood the engine in the normal way in heavy rain on the Chester bypass but the first really memorable occurrence was going up the A5 during the night. I was driving and Ted was asleep by my side. As we reached the brow of a hill I found that I was confronted by two car transporters with no room for me. Luckily there was a grass verge and although several inches high I managed to get up this without any damage except Ted's sleep. Heart pounding, the first thing I heard was Ted saying, 'You rotten sod, what did you do that for!'

Anyway, we carried on, had our rest and breakfast and eventually joined the queue waiting to enter the Aintree circuit. After a few minutes a police motorcycle patrol slowed down beside me and beckoned me to follow him. I don't know if he thought he had recognised me as someone important or whether he was just having some fun but he led me right down the outside of the queue on the wrong side of the road and the wrong side of the traffic islands to the head of the queue, held back the cars already entering and waved me in. Then with a cheery wave off he went!

Coming back after an enjoyable race we were held up in the approach to the Mersey Tunnel while the police removed a broken-down car. Being the first in the queue when the tunnel re-opened I let rip and made the most magnificent noise as we came through. The rest of the journey was uneventful except for more flooding of the engine with water as soon as it started raining.

Next came the 1958 Exeter Trial, again accompanied by Ted, consisting of muddy hill-climbs connected by road sections. All went well until on one hill-climb stage, we not only knocked off half of the exhaust system, but also came to an undignified stop as we approached the top and had to be rescued by a tractor. We therefore decided that retirement was called for but carried on to stay the rest of the weekend at the pub we knew well at Dittisham on the banks of the River Dart.

After this came various rallies always consisting of a series of timed driving tests of the manoeuvring in and out of garages type in which I always did quite well, but never won anything. The most memorable of these was the Eastbourne Rally which included driving tests in the car park at the top of Beachy Head and more on the sea front at Eastbourne.

Although under normal conditions it was a beautiful gear change, it was not easy to get from first to reverse and vice versa in a hurry, and it was playing havoc with my gearboxes. This was why I was so glad of my previous experience in rebuilding them, but eventually and regretfully, I came to the conclusion that the Jupiter had to go. This conclusion had come about because there had been an occasion when the strain on the gear-change column became apparent by deciding to break at the most inconvenient moment leaving me with no gears. We managed a temporary repair – I don't remember how – but at least we were able to get back home again.

I then bought a 1956 Ford Zephyr convertible and sold the Jupiter but I don't remember how much I got for it or where it went. This went some way towards improving my competition performance, but I was still not winning!

However, when I traded in the Zephyr against a new Austin Healey Sprite when they first appeared at the end of 1958, things changed dramatically because the first event I entered in it, which I think was the 1959 Brighton Rally, I at last had success by winning the novice's award. I also ran it in the Brighton Speed Trials with a much-modified engine and easily beat the Triumph TR2 which I ran alongside, finishing the run at over 100 mph. I enjoyed driving the Zephyr for the short time that I had it, but it was hardly a sports car.

I had no more personal involvement with Jowetts after that apart from saying that my sister-in-law, Beryl, who lives in Burgh Heath in Surrey had a Javelin for a short time, and when a work colleague, Alan Dove, who lived in the Lewisham area of South London asked me to vet a Javelin for him that he was thinking of buying. It was a good one, so he bought it but I must confess I do not have any details for either of these cars. There was also an acquaintance of Ted's from the Bull Inn at Clandon in Surrey who we used to see racing his Morris Minor at Goodwood. He had shoe-horned a Jupiter engine into this. It was a tight but very good fit and when he took part in handicap races he was always on scratch, competing on equal terms with cars such as big Jaguars.

You may also be interested to know that a few Jupiter chassis were bought by a small coach-building shop in Wimbledon where, although their main business was accident repair, they had very nice hand-built bodies fitted. I don't know what happened to these, as I never saw them again.

This I regret is the end of the Jowett saga, after having a lot of fun (and expense), mostly with Ted's help and sometimes with my brother Geoff, I settled down to a quiet, and shortly to be, married life which, I am thankful to say, still continues.

In the intervening years I have had some interesting cars including Jaguar and Triumph Stag, which I think was a very underrated car. It was reasonably fast and had good all-round performance. The road holding was interesting to say the least until one got used to it. They had a reputation for engine trouble caused

This Jupiter registered PTT243 was owned by Brian Hearn in the early 1950s. This picture shows him taking part in the 1954 Exeter Trial coming up Strete's Hill. This was the last hill climb he did in the car, as it was damaging the underside of it. He thought that the car was not designed for this kind of treatment. He retired to the local pub at Dittisham, a small village on the banks of the River Dart, where he was made very welcome! (Hearne)

by overheating, but if one kept the radiator clean they (at least, mine) gave no trouble.

I now have somewhat more mundane transport in the shape of a 1995 Vauxhall Cavalier Expression 1.8, which was the last Cavalier model produced and was something of a special edition and has such things as alloy wheels and various other luxuries. It has a surprisingly good performance and would easily out-perform any standard Jupiter, but it is not quite the same thing! However, it is not allowed in my garage, as this is occupied by my wife's Peugeot 106 and my son's 3.3-litre BMW Coupé. Say no more!

Brian Hearn ... Lower Kingswood, Tadworth, Surrey, January 2004

JUPITER REGISTERED JUN592

My father, who was a doctor, had two Javelins, the first being a more basic specification, or earlier car which was registered HNM744, beige in colour, which he purchased used in part-exchange for an Austin A40 Devon. This will have been in about 1949 and I think he paid about £800 for it.

This Jupiter, chassis number E3/SA/898 and registered JUN592, was bought in 1954 by a doctor who owned two Javelins. He bought the car for his son, Max Trimble, to rally and race. He did this for about a year or so until he suffered a broken crankshaft. This picture was taken of Max in action at Silverstone on Saturday 21 April 1954. (Trimble)

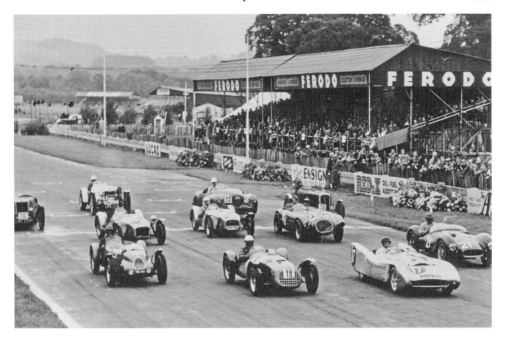

Also taken at Silverstone on Saturday 21 April 1954, at the start of the race. After parting with the car, Max moved onto an Austin Healey 100 and subsequently Jaguar C and D Types. He had wanted to obtain a Jupiter R1 but was not able to. (Trimble)

A mystery picture (to me) taken in France in the late 1950s or early 1960s showing a Jupiter parked next to a much earlier Bugatti.

A really nice publicity shot for the American market showing an attractive girl with an SA Jupiter.

He then bought a brand new Javelin in 1953 which was coloured connaught green; it was purchased from the local Jowett agent in Birmingham and was registered NOK199. This was a great car and was to a much higher specification than the first car.

In 1954 my father bought a 1953 Jupiter mainly for me to drive and also to rally and race, which I did for about a year until the crankshaft broke at Goodwood! After that I continued racing, but with an Austin Healey 100 and subsequently Jaguar C & D Type cars.

I would have liked at that time to have got hold of an R1 Jupiter, but that was not to be. I have about three pictures of the Jupiter in action if you would like to borrow them. Unfortunately I do not have any pictures of either of the Javelins, nor do I have any other data relating to these cars – all lost in the mists of time! But I do remember on one occasion going to the factory in Bradford with my father, but I do not remember now what we went there for.

Max Trimble ... Droitwich, Worcs, February 2001

Needless to say, I wrote to Max to ask to borrow the pictures of his Jupiter whilst racing, the car turned out to be JUN592, a late Mark 1 model, chassis number E3/SA/898/R. He raced the car at Goodwood and Silverstone during 1954.

JUPITER JBE4

After buying my Jupiter registered JBE4 in February 1985, I spent some time on trying to trace the car's earlier history, as I only had a continuation log book which started in 1967. I managed to contact Bill Jarrett, who owned it in the mid-1960s. After speaking to him on the phone, he sent me this most enjoyable letter:

I bought my Jowett Jupiter one dark night in November 1966, as a 'going concern', from Christopher Parkes, but in a rather tatty condition. It was my first Jowett and I used it on journeys to and from work, which amounted to 15 miles a day. I was a bit wary of it due to overheard conversations at various club meetings regarding broken crankshafts and suspect head gaskets etc. The only problem I had was with a thrust washer in the gearbox. I built up a new one from two spare boxes that came with the car; I also fitted new bearings at that time. The only problem I had with this box was when I managed to jam it trying to find reverse outside The Green Man in Ealing, which entailed me taking the side panel off to sort things out. I could only find first gear, so had to drive seven miles home at 15 miles per hour with no undue overheating, so I was greatly relieved. Another problem that I had, which I feel I should mention, was when the passenger door blew off in a gale! I managed to retrieve it and refit it when I got home, but it was a draughty drive back!

I re-sprayed the car in BMC red, as this was as close as I could get to the original Jowett colour. I also had the bumpers re-chromed, so the car was starting to look quite tidy. The seat was also in a poor way, the leather having dried and cracked, and with a lot of stitching missing. When I was looking at cars in the local scrap yard I spotted a 1958 2.4 Jaguar with an excellent rear seat in navy blue. I bought it for £2 and it gave me enough leather to recover the Jupiter front seat. Soon after this I had an unfortunate experience, when the car was stolen by joy riders, just after I had completed the re-spray; the car ended up against a wall with damage to the front wing and chassis member. The insurance company took care of the repairs, after I had located a second-hand front wing for the car; so the moral of the story is to not leave your keys in the ignition with the car pointing down a hill!

I decided to take the car to the Jowett Car Club National Rally in Harrogate in 1967; I set off from Berkhampstead on the Saturday morning at 10 o'clock, picking up a friend on the way. We passed through Leighton Buzzard and Bedford to the A1, and after about 100 miles of trouble-free motoring at 60-65 mph, we stopped for a snack and a check of the car. We had used about half a pint of water, but everything else was OK so we pushed on, with no trouble, to our destination. We checked into the hotel, which was a very good choice, and had a meal. The next day we parked the car on the Stray in Harrogate with all the other Jowetts. As this was our first rally, we enjoyed the exchange of views with other club members very much. I was also greatly encouraged by the condition of the car, as it looked better than several on display.

As the car had performed so well on the way to Harrogate, we decided to go across to Rhyl in North Wales to visit some friends. This trip was uneventful, and the only problem I had was with the wiring of the horn, as it tooted every time I made a right turn, I soon sorted this out on my return.

We set off from Rhyl to Berkhampstead mid-afternoon; on the motorway the car boiled over as the bottom hose had gone. I managed to make a temporary repair using insulation tape, but I had no water to fill the radiator again. By this time it was dark, so we were a bit stuck; my friend noticed we were parked next to a manhole cover, which was to save the day. We lifted it up; climbed down inside and filled up a bottle with water out of it several times until the radiator was full. We set off again for Berkhampstead and arrived home with no other problems; we covered a total of 535 miles during the trip, with the hood down all the time! With hindsight, it is amazing what we did in our cars in those days. There is not much chance of doing that now!

Bill Jarrett … formally of Berkhampstead, 1986

JUPITER JBE4

The owner of the car prior to Bill Jarrett was Christopher Parkes of 48 Lambs Conduit Street, London WC1, who owned the car from August to December 1965, but I was not able to trace him. By chance, several Northern Section members of the Jowett Car Club went on holiday to the Isle of Man in their cars in the early 1990s. At one stage, the cars (which included a Jupiter) were parked on the sea front and a gentleman came up and said, 'I used to own one of these.' To cut a long story short, it was Christopher Parkes!

I managed to locate Christopher Parkes in the Isle of Man, using directory enquires; he told me that at that time he was a student based in London. He lived at the London address, which was a flat, during the week, but went back to his parents' home in Oxford most weekends. He had been running a very smart SC Jupiter, but he had several problems with it. The main being a recurring problem where the gear change kept fracturing. This had been welded up several times. The killer blow for this car was when the clutch burnt out, as he could not afford to have a new one fitted, so he sold the car as it stood to a person in London.

He then bought JBE4 with the proceeds, which was a running car, but very scruffy in comparison. At least he was back on the road again, but not for long! It was soon apparent that the engine was in very poor condition. He managed to find some second-hand pistons in a scrapyard out of a Javelin, but these were not successful, so he decided to do the job properly. He bought a Javelin engine from the same scrapyard and rebuilt it with proper Jupiter pistons. When it was ready to be fitted, he bought a cheap block and tackle to lift out the old engine and put in the replacement. This was fitted with nylon ropes, rather than the usual chains, so he expected this to be easier to use. This proved not to be the case, as the nylon ropes jammed in the pulley under the weight of the engine. He got round that by attaching the nylon ropes to his friend's Hillman Imp back bumper, and drove it forwards to gain the height to lift it over the front chassis member.

While he was rebuilding the engine, he left the car parked on the street and worked on various parts on the kitchen table in the flat. Needless to say, this did not impress his new bride! Once the new engine was installed, he decided to sell the car. It was rather vulnerable parked outside on a London street, as it was so easy to gain access to it. He advertised the car and sold it to Bill Jarrett for £25.

This transaction was less than straightforward, as Christopher had agreed to drive the car to Bill's address, so the car could be inspected prior to purchase. He was slowing down to go round a small roundabout, but lost control of the car, he drove over the top of the roundabout before he could bring it to a halt. The car was not damaged, but the loss of control was due to the driver's side front wheel 'developing a mind of its own'. The split pin at the track-rod end had dropped out to cause this. He soon had the car jacked up and fitted another; he then continued on to Bill Jarrett and completed the transaction, with Bill being none the wiser! Christopher felt he had been very lucky, as this had happened when he was slowing down in a 30 mph area. He said that if it had happened shortly before, when he was travelling at speed, it would have been a very different story.

He moved to Castletown, Isle of Man, in 1974. He lived there until 1980, when he moved to his present address in Peel. [*Taken from a phone call with Christopher Parkes … NS*]

Also available from Amberley Publishing

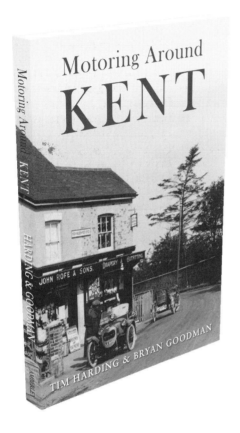

Motoring Around Kent
Tim Harding & Bryan Goodman
ISBN: 978-1-84868-575-8
Price: £12.99

Available from all good bookshops, or order direct
from our website www.amberleybooks.com